The Public Subscription Windmill

and

The Round House at Lewes

With many thanks
for all your help.
Annie

The Story of the People who Lived,
Owned and Worked in these Buildings

ANNIE CROWTHER

THIS BOOK IS DEDICATED TO THE SMART AND SHELLEY FAMILIES
AND TO MY BELOVED PARENTS, JOE AND LILIAS CROWTHER

First published in 2001 by Pipe Passage Books, Lewes

ISBN 0 9541462 04

Typeset by JEM Editorial, jemedit@aol.com

Printed and bound by Tansleys the Printers
19 Broad Street
Seaford
Sussex BN25 1LS
telephone: 01323 891019

CONTENTS

Front cover: *The front of the Round House painted by Susan Ridler*

Inside front and back covers: *Words and music of the Dusty Miller song*

INTRODUCTION

The year 2001 marks the bicentennial of the building of the Public Subscription Wind Corn Mill in Lewes. To mark this event, I would like to share with you the history of the windmill, the Round House, its situation and the people who have lived and worked here in its almost two hundred years' existence.

The families referred to are made up from very ordinary people, whose stories are rarely documented. I hope to make them 'stars of their ordinariness'. I, too am part of the history and I would like to write about my influences on the property and my love affair with it and its previous residents. Although the mill and The Round House have been well documented in books, articles, maps and talks on windmills, and referred to in books about Leonard and Virginia Woolf and other members of the Bloomsbury group, there is nothing that tells of it as a place of work and as a home.

This book is not a definitive document of the history of this site. Its history is unfolding all the time and is not just in the past. I cannot claim academic expertise in social history, industrial history, literature or archaeology. All I can offer is my insatiable interest in these subjects and a desire to present an informal essay on the history of the Public Subscription Windmill, and the subsequent history of The Round House and the families who have lived and worked there. My Round House would like to share with you its many interesting stories, its encounters, its feelings, its sounds, its smells and its sights and visions.

During my research at the Sussex Archaeological Society's library at the Barbican I came across this piece, written in 1804 by John Button Junior in honour of *The Lewes Library Society*. I do hope that I am not being too presumptuous in comparing myself with Mr Button but I feel that his poem reflects my attitude to this book.

To Celebrate this Society, the Author has employed his late hours of Leisure. Commenced in a frolic, written at intervals and without the slightest view to publication, the Poem has length swelled to its present size. To his Subscribers he returns his warmest thanks, not the unmeaning bow of cold civility, but the effects of feelings which gush from a heart that beats with gratitude and respect.

If you pass the Round House and I am available, I will be most pleased to share the experience of living in this delightful house.

Annie Crowther
The Round House, Lewes
October 2001

ONE

THE HISTORY OF THE SITE

Not far from the coast, where the land suddenly becomes bare and chalky and folds itself into humps and hollows; where the wind from the south-west often tastes salt, and a herring-gull on the roof-tops is no uncommon sight, stands a Little Town.
Eve Garnett

The Round House, as it is now known, previously Smart's Mill then Shelley's Mill, and originally the Public Subscription Wind Corn Mill, was built in 1801-2 – but what of the earlier history of the site, and the twitten in which it is situated? The land lying behind the medieval Town Wall, running westwards along the perimeter of the Round House site, was part of the area of the town's defences that were once patrolled by the Saxon sentries. Looking up at dusk, from the Westgate car park, scanning the impressive height of the

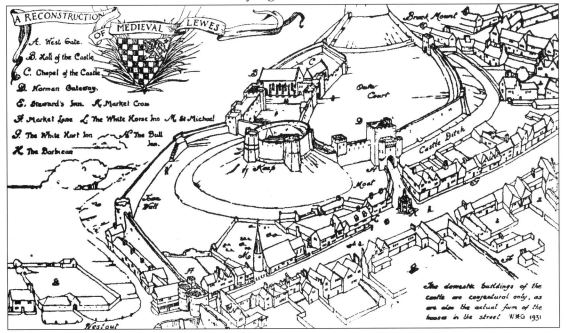

WH Godfrey's 1931 reconstruction of medieval Lewes, showing the tower on the Town Wall.

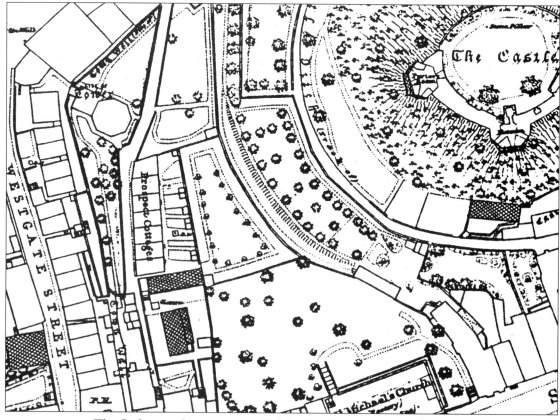

The Ordnance Survey map of 1873, showing the site of the tower.

wall and allowing the imagination to run wild, it is just possible to imagine the Saxons guarding against marauders waiting to attack through the West Gate of this heavily fortified town.

The remaining sections of the town wall rise up behind Keere Street to the site of the West Gate, and descend behind the garden of the Round house in Pipe Passage and Castle Banks to Abinger Place and St John sub Castro. There is debate as to the circuit of the rest of the town wall and it remains uncertain whether any stone wall existed on the east of the town where the river protected the approach.

The Ordnance Survey map of 1873, WH Godfrey's reconstructed plan and map of the Town Wall, and his historical notes on Lewes Castle, indicate the site of a tower on the west side of the town wall that borders the garden of the Round House. The tower has been lost under an extension built on to the Round House in 1927.

Much of the upper part of the Town Wall is still intact, but the lower part has suffered the ravages of time. Myrtle Broadbent, a previous occupant of the Round House who lived here with her parents, recalls that at about nine o'clock on the night of March 2, 1940, the sitting room started to shake and then a dull roaring sound was heard. Her father and Mac, an evacuee schoolmaster billeted with the family during the Second World War, went out with torches to investigate what had happened. To their horror, they discovered that much of the Town Wall had collapsed into Westgate. As a result of the substantial damage, the council was forced to take emergency remedial action to shore up the side of the house and the wall. The two large rooms in the house, the sitting room and the main bedroom, were placed out of bounds for nine months until the wall was repaired with brick reinforcement.

Unfortunately, much of the old flint of the ancient Town Wall was lost and, because it was wartime, little was done to reinstate it correctly. As a result of the negligent repair, much of the top of the wall is, today, still in urgent need of proper attention. Miss Broadbent said her mother believed that the collapse of the wall was a result of slum clearance in White Lion Lane (now known as Westgate), which had taken place in 1939, rather than war damage.

A recently discovered terracotta plaque in the back garden of the Round House reveals much earlier damage to the Town Wall. It reads:

A PORTION OF
THE TOWN WALL
BUILT ABOUT A. D. 1150
REPAIRED BY
"MURAGE" GRANTS
A. D. 1245-1345

Murage was a tax levied to build and maintain town walls. Thomas Horsfield, in *The History and Antiquities of Lewes and its Vicinity*, gives an explanation of the murage grant and how the tax was levied in 1266 and in 1334. The town, Horsfield wrote, had been severely damaged in the Battle of Lewes in 1264.

In 1265-6 Lord Warrene, having regained his land and properties, successfully requested permission of Henry III to impose tolls and taxes on goods entering and being sold within the town, the duties to be levied by the Constables. The list of tolls is extensive and now offers a fascinating insight into the range of goods available in the Middle Ages.

The collapsed wall pictured in March 1940.

A farthing for every thousand of herrings for sale, a half-penny for every load of garlic for sale, a half-penny for every millstone for sale, a penny for ten sheep or hogs for sale, a penny for every dozen of cordovans for sale.

There is no indication of how much money was raised from these taxes in the three years that they were charged, but it was not sufficient. Seventy years later, in 1334, with fears of a French invasion, Edward III authorised further tolls for restoration to the town's wall defences, to be levied for a further five years. This time the range of goods was more sophisticated.

For every cloth of silk and gold, satin and diaper and embroidered silk, a half-penny, for every hundred of linen thread, canvas, Irish cloth, and worsted, for sale, a penny, for every lamprey for sale before Easter, a farthing . . . for every hundred of lamb, kid, hare rabbit, fox, cat and squirrel skins for sale, a half-penny.

The earth bank to the rear of the Round House, running parallel with the town wall, is a long triangular strip that could possibly be an ancient tumuli, a conjecture of historian John Bleach, although, to date,

The Town Wall below The Round House (seen top left); picturesque, but in urgent need of restoration.

there is no corroborating evidence to back this up. John Houghton, in his book *Unknown Lewes*, writes that the land was, perhaps – 'earth removed from the castle's south western motte, and deposited on top of the old Anglo-Saxon boundaries'.

In 1993, when I bought the Round House, much work was needed to make this long patch of land more manageable. I asked if the Sussex Archeological Society would be willing to excavate the land before it was set to lawn. Sadly,

there were not the financial resources to undertake a major dig. However, under the auspices of Liz Somerville and David Gregory, a training exercise was undertaken in February 1994. The garden yielded some pottery sherds, possibly from medieval kilns in Ringmer. Dr Richard Jones and David Gregory carried out a further excavation in 1995. This followed the discovery of a large animal jaw bone when foundations were being laid for a new retaining wall. Examination was made of the soil strata and six deposits were identified. Sixty pieces of pottery – undecorated, unglazed and wheel-thrown – were retrieved.

Both digs suggest a probable Saxo-Norman date for the pottery (tenth to eleventh centuries). This would challenge John Houghton's theory that the earth was deposited from the excavation of the second motte on the Anglo-Saxon defences.

A large range of animal bones was found, evidently from a more recent date, and the conclusion was that the site was a domestic one and the bones were deposited when butcher William Smith used the site in the late eighteenth century. The bones were of cattle, pig, domestic fowl, sheep and goat. Some of the bones showed signs of butchery cuts and other had been gnawed by dogs.

In 1624 the parcel of land covering the area north of what is now New Road, south to the High Street, including 151 and 152 High Street, the Town Wall to the west and east to the Castle Ditch, was owned by John Bray of Balcombe and tenanted by John French. In 1626, the parish records of St Michael show the freeholder as his son, Henry Braye (or Bray), a yeoman of Balcombe. In 1665, Henry Braye granted a lease on the land, which included a messuage, shops, cellars, gardens and an orchard, to John David, of Lewes, a turner. The occupiers were given then as the Widow Jeanes and others. The freehold passed down the family to Mildred Bray, a widow and her son, Henry, who sold the lease of the properties to John Peckham for £100, on March 20 and 21, 1712. At that date, the occupiers were Rebecca Jones, widow, Samuel Jones, John Gilham, Nicholas Brown, Thomas Ayres and Henry Rose.

On July 18, 1721, John Peckham mortgaged the land and properties for £100 to John Holmwood, of the Cliffe, apothecary, and John Dungate of Southover, mercer. The term was to be 1,000 years and a peppercorn rent was charged. On June 8, 1723, a tripartite indenture for the plot was arranged between John Holmwood and John Dungate, John Peckham, and Mary Gard, spinster, of Southover, On March 25, 1734, Mary Gard assigned her share of the mortgage to William Brett, of Lewes,

apothecary, for a further charge of £100. On April 23, 1737, the land and property was conveyed by John Peckham to Thomas Pelham for £50, the mortgage of £150, granted by William Brett, was paid off and a sum of £200 paid to John Peckham by Thomas Pelham. This is a rather potted history but it does locate some of the known figures of the seventeenth and eighteenth century

It is worth noting here that in 1768

A view along Pipe Passage to the Round House, c1961, when Prospect Cottages were undergoing restoration.

9

A glimpse of Lewes High Street
from Pipe Passage, taken from In and Out
and Roundabout by Eve Garnett.

Thomas Pelham succeeded to the Barony of Stanmer on the death of the Duke of Newcastle. He was also created Earl of Chichester on June 23, 1801. In 1802, the same land was leased to the 'Subscribers to the Public Corn Wind Mill' and was known as Smith's Croft, as previously a lease had been granted to William Smith, butcher, by Lord Pelham.

Ann, Dowager Countess of Chichester, sold the freehold of the site in 1810 to Robert Neal, on the death of her husband the Earl of Chichester. Until 1812 the site was known as the Town Mill. It passed briefly to John Lade and, in 1814, the mill became known as Smart's Mill.

In the 1841 census, the passage from New Road to the High Street was identified as 'Western Terrace'. The parish records of 1846 reveal that an illegitimate daughter was born to Mary Deadman in 'Pipe Alley' and another birth is recorded in 'Clock Alley'. Were these alternative names for the twitten?

On the death of Robert Neal, in 1855, his executors offered his properties for sale by auction at the White Hart, in March of the same year. The row of seven cottages east of the Mill House was catalogued as 'Prospect Row', the name chosen to denote that the properties had the benefit of a panoramic view to the west of the town as well wonderful views of the castle. The baptismal registers of the 1860s refer to the property as the 'Round House in Pipes Passage'.

Why Pipe Alley? Why Pipes Passage? The name was adopted when clay pipes began to be manufactured in the passage in the 1830s. The clay pipe industry had started and grown in Lewes from the late seventeenth century, when a plentiful supply of clay was brought up the river

Ouse and landed in Lewes. Early pipe makers included Richard Briant, Richard Flayde and John Holcom and, in the eighteenth century, Thomas Harman and his sons John and Thomas. By 1800, the Harman and Neeve families were both working at 99 High Street and Henry Pink, John Tanner and Charles Bishop were using a kiln in Keere Street. The continuing demand for pipes resulted in a kiln being constructed at the rear of the Masonic Lodge, in the twitten that then became known as Pipes Passage.

Norman Norris carried out an excavation of the kiln in 1956 and his papers (*A Victorian Pipe Kiln in Lewes*) are lodged with the Sussex Archaeological Society library. He found evidence of a large covered kiln that was replaced by a smaller one when pipe smoking started to decline. Finds in the kiln dated from 1830 to about 1880 and pipes made by Pink, Corner, Hartington and John Tucknot were unearthed. It is commonly believed that John Tucknot collected damaged pipes from local hostelries, including the very popular long stemmed pipes known as a churchwardens. These were cleaned and repaired in the Pipe Passage kiln and this may account for the differently-named pipes discovered during the excavation. The smoking of this type of pipe had a ceremonial role in that they were smoked after the swearing in of churchwardens.

The little twitten has had other names. In the 1871 census the passage reverted to Western Terrace. By the 1891 census, the round house was known as the Mill House, located in Western Passage. In 1919 Virginia Woolf wrote in her diary that the Round House was to be found in 'Pipes Passage'. The Ordnance Survey map of 1921 again gives the address as Western Terrace, as did John Every's planning application for the Round House, submitted in 1927.

The see-sawing of the name continued until 1938, when Pipes lost its 's' and the byway became Pipe Passage. All too often, when a piece of animal bone pushes its way to the surface in the garden, I remember that I really live on Smith's Croft.

In *Sussex Cottage* Esther Meynell encapsulated the specialness of this almost hidden Lewes twitten. She wrote:

Not far away from this house (Bull House), but on the other side of the road, is a curious little narrow passage, so small and squashed that one may pass it a dozen times without notice. It is one of the little secret places of Lewes and worth exploring: Its narrow entry and steep steps have something to show. Like many old towns, and perhaps more than most, Lewes has a certain magic, and at some hours and seasons it seems that the past steals back. On a cold spring evening, with the sky still bright, but the ground growing dusky, walk up the narrow deserted Pipe's Passage, and past the oddly placed greenhouses of a market-gardener you will see the Keep from an unaccustomed side. Look long enough in the evening stillness, and it is not impossible that you will see a figure lean over the battlements – you are not quite sure, but it looks like a lady with a high pointed head-dress from which a wisp of veil flutters faintly. She waves her hand – who to? Certainly not to you.

TWO

THE PUBLIC SUBSCRIPTION WIND CORN MILL

The Public Subscription Wind Corn Mill built in Lewes is thought to be the only corn mill erected in Sussex for public use. It came about because of a dire need for decent food, particularly wheat, for the poor of the town. Two forces had affected the supply – the Napoleonic Wars between 1793 and 1815, which resulted in a sharp fall in the amount of corn being imported from Europe, causing cereal prices to escalate sharply; and the harvest failure in 1795 and continued poor conditions through to 1800. In 1799 there was heavy and prolonged rain in the harvest months of August and September and two nights of heavy frost in mid-October. As a result wheat had died off at the root before it had time to ripen and much of it was not worth harvesting.

Local landowners were aware that people were going hungry and this, coupled with an outbreak of smallpox in Lewes, caused an air of discontent to fester. In the winter of 1794-5, as a result of the bitter weather, 1,000 of the town's poor had been fed a rich pea broth donated by Thomas Kemp, the wool merchant – a duty that he continued in the following year, adding meat to the broth to make it more substantial.

In 1800 wheat cost '112 shillings and ten pence a pound'. The spring was late and cold and although early summer promised well, the heavy rains set in again, as in the previous year. The crops harvested were coarse and scant and barely fit for human consumption. There was a growing fear that the food riots, already occurring elsewhere in the country, would escalate into revolution as witnessed across the Channel in France. An anonymous letter from Uckfield, read at the Lewes Corn Exchange, fuelled this fear. The letter warned of armed insurrection if the price of corn was not lowered.

In a desperate measure to control the unrest and avert the shortage of food, particularly cereal crops, a series of Acts were passed by the government :

January, 1800 – *An Act for enabling His Majesty to prohibit the Exportation of Bread and permit the Importation of Corn.*

February, 1800 – *An Act to Prohibit until the Expiration of 6 weeks after the Commencement of the next session of Parliament, any person or persons from selling any Bread which shall not have been baked at a Certain Time.*

March, 1800 – *An Act to prohibit, until the first Day of October one thousand eight hundred the use of Wheat in the Making of Starch.*

December, 1800 – *An Act for Granting Bounties on the Importation of Wheat, Barley, Rye, Oats, Pease, Beans and Indian Corn and of Barley and Indian Meal and Wheaten Flour and Rice.*

The Bread Act, also passed in December 1800, set out to control the food eaten by the poor in the workhouse and those on parish relief:

An Act for making better Provision for the Maintenance of the Poor and for the Diminishing of Bread Corn by directing the Manner of applying Parish Relief until the sixth day of one thousand eight hundred and one and from thence until the End of Six weeks after the Meeting of the next Session of Parliament.

Plans were made to substitute alternative foodstuffs into the meagre diets of the inhabitants of the workhouses and those on parish relief. Overseers who failed to implement this policy were brought before the magistrates, warned that they must start the new feeding regimes immediately and were told to report back to General Quarter Sessions the savings they had made on cereals.

In the *Sussex Weekly Advertiser*, the corn chandlers at Lewes Corn Exchange reported, on Friday, 26 September, 1800:

Since Monday, Scarce a single vessel has arrived at market; the remains of that day's sale of English wheat is very coarse and indifferent, that the mealmen do not appear to take it off, at even reduced prices; whilst best samples of foreign wheat are on the advance.

A memorandum was set out in *The Town Book of Lewes*, in the summer of 1800, to the effect that a public mill would be built by subscription:

PUBLICK CORN MILL. Waited on the Duke of Norfolk, for the Purpose of obtaining of His Grace, to the extent of his Claim, a Grant of the Brake Mount, whereon to erect, by Subscription a Public Windmill; but His Grace having thought proper to reject the Application the Mill is forthwith to be erected in Smith's Croft, an eligible Spot, near the Southern Boundary of the Castle Precinct, by value of a Grant from Lord Pelham , on a long Lease, at a trifling annual Rent. The Mill is contracted for at Six Hundred Pounds independent of the Round House, which the Subscribers are to build at their own cost from the Foundation one Foot above the Surface, all below being included in the Contract. The hope of obtaining genuine Meal without the Fear of Adulteration for the use of the Inhabitants of the Borough was the Origin of this Plan, and more especially as at this time of Dearth, it regards the Poor most essentially.

It was further reported:

FLOUR of very bad quality at the Time of making these Minutes was, occasioned by the War and Monopoly, more than by actual Scarcity, sold at Three Shillings and Twopence a Gallon owing to the extravagant Price of wheat which was from Forty to Forty -four Pound a Load; other Grain in proportion and Hay from six to eight Pounds a ton.

The Constables were aware of:

BREAD. Short of Weight, Much found on frequently visiting the Bakers. Seized the light Loaves, and occasioned the Defaulters to be fined.

As a result of these irregular weights and measures, it was demanded that these should be seized and burnt in the public market place and new, accurate weights and measures put into use. Liquid measures, as used in inns and public houses, coal measures and shop weighing scales that were found to be illegal, were seized and destroyed.

The Constables, keen to be seen in control of the situation, instructed men to collect all of the illegal weights and measures and to destroy them on a bonfire, so that the townsfolk could witness their destruction. New, accurate sets of measures to be used in shops and hostelries where food or drink was sold were to be mandatory. Surviving illegal measures that had escaped the purge were to be seized and their owners heavily fined.

These actions were strongly enforced by the Constables, William Lee and John Baker, in an attempt to prevent any civil disobedience and rioting by the people. There appeared to be a genuine concern for the plight of the poor and, mindful of the feeling of unrest in the town, Sir Thomas Carr, the High Sheriff, used the Town Hall to sell flour at eighteen pence a gallon – 'to the poor and inferior mechanics of the town', according to Horsfield. This was less than half the price it had been sold at previously, so was much welcomed by the needy. *The Town Book of Lewes* records that the efforts of the Constables were to be commended, and thanks were offered to them by the Reverend George Jenkyns of St Michael's church.

The plan to erect a public mill was taken a step further with an announcement in the *Sussex Weekly Advertiser*, on September 20, 1800.

To Mill Wrights. A Public Wind Corn Mill being intended to be built within the Borough of Lewes, capable of working two pairs of stones, of the dimensions of 4ft 6ins to 5ft, with a bolter completely fitted for use, such mill wrights as wish to engage in building the same, are requested to deliver in Plans and Estimates of Expense of Wind Corn Mill of descriptions and of the above to Mr. William Lee and Mr. John Baker, Constables of the Borough of Lewes on or before the committee appointed to consider the same, which meeting shall be holden at the Star Inn in Lewes, on Tuesday the 7th day of October next, at the hour of six in the evening.

On October 9 a further announcement was made in the newspaper.

TO MILLWRIGHTS.
A COMMITTEE appointed to carry into execution a proposition for erecting a PUBLIC CORN WINDMILL for the use of the inhabitants of the Borough of Lewes met, by adjournment, at the Star Inn, in the said Borough, on the 7th inst.
'UNAMIMOUSLY RESOLVED,
That a Smock Wind Corn Mill should be erected on the Bray Mount, and that £600, and no more should be expended erecting such Mill, including a permanent foundation, on which the same is to be erected; to be fitted up with two pair of French Burr stones, for grinding Wheaten Flour, with Boulter and all her gear

complete, and fit for working by the 14th June next.

Millwrights willing to contract for the building and fitting up the same, are requested to deliver their proposals to Messrs LEE and BAKER, of Lewes on or before the 21st inst. Accompanied with a plan and full specification of the dimensions of all working gear and scantlings, in order that the same may be laid before the Committee at their next Meeting, at the Star Inn, on Friday, the 24th inst. At the hour of six in the evening precisely, where they are requested to attend to explain the merits of their respective plans.
LANGRIDGE and KELL SECRETARIES

As reported in *The Town Book of Lewes*, and despite the grave urgency, the Duke of Norfolk, owner of Bray Mound (now known as Brack Mound or Mount) opposed the plan to build a windmill on his land. His refusal caused mounting concern and delayed the plan to build the windmill. The *Sussex Weekly Advertiser* continued to draw attention to the suffering of the poor, reporting on November 24, 1800:

Though wheat last week experienced a considerable drop in the London Markets it sold higher than on the preceding market day, and *The necessity of the public corn mill was nevermore strongly evinced than at this place, on Saturday last, when the inhabitants experienced so great a lack of flour, that none could be had for money till a late hour in the evening.*

A letter sent to the newspaper was of the opinion that the scarcity did not exist, or at best, had been deliberately inflated to give an artificial price for cereals.
At our market on Saturday, we are concerned to state, that wheat rose in price, though the experience of every day serves more and more to satisfy the public, that there is no actual scarcity. To what end have importations encouraged and procured? Or to what purpose have the exertions of Government, in other respects been used is this alarming evil to continue? Let but a MAXIMUM be fixed, and the BUGBEAR scarcity, will soon vanish, or be exposed to shame.

Another view expressed in the *Advertiser* blamed the shortage on the practice of amalgamating smaller farms into larger units by landowners who could afford to withhold their cereals from the markets to dictate the prices. Whatever the reason for the shortage, one thing can be sure, it was the poor that suffered.

On December 22, 1800, the newspaper reported:

It is proved by the evidence of the books of several bakers, in this town, that the Poor consume a much larger quantity of flour in times of Dearth, than in the times of PLENTY! We are grieved to state, that wheat experienced another considerable rise in price at our market on Saturday, where the best samples fetched £38 per load.
'The angry scourge of Providence, seems every day to fall with additional weight, and we fear, MOST heavily, on those who least provoke it, namely the inferior Tradesmen and Mechanics, who are tottering amidst their HALF STARVED families, looking for relief to that state alone, which gives equal Rank to KINGS and BEGGARS.

Representations were made to Lord Pelham to ask for his help in finding a suitable site for the mill. He agreed to

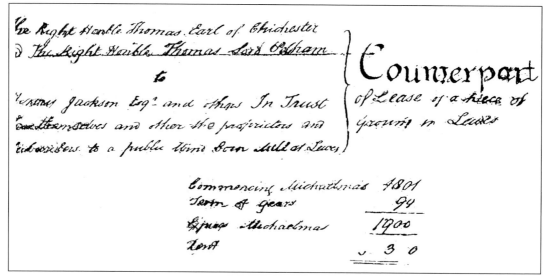

Lease granted by Thomas, Earl of Chichester, and his son, Thomas, Lord Pelham, to the committee of the Public Subscription Wind Corn Mill.

grant a lease on a parcel of land known as Smith's Croft, for the erection of the new mill. In the preceding chapter the early ownership of the site was given up until 1747, when Lord Pelham bought the freehold from John and Sarah Peckham.

As freeholders of Smith's Croft, Thomas, Earl of Chichester, and Thomas, Lord Pelham, granted a lease to Henry Jackson of Lewes; William Franklin Hick of Lewes, gentleman; William Balcombe Langridge, gentleman; William Lee, printer; John Bray Cater, brandy merchant; George Wille, builder; Joseph Goldsmith, builder; Charles Wille, builder and John Whiteman, blacksmith. These were elected members of a committee to oversee the building of the mill, in trust for themselves and the other proprietors. Presumably the builders on the committee, George Wille, his son Charles Wille and Joseph Goldsmith, were entrusted with the construction of the round house, and John Whiteman, blacksmith, with the machinery of the

windmill. John Whiteman was listed, in 1795, as using the forge in Fisher Street, where it is still located.

Pilbeam was the millwright employed to construct the smock. A later report in the newspaper stated that he was a local man, but little is known about him and no reference to him can be found in the many books written on windmills. There is a possibility that he was 'Pilbeam of Chailey'. The *Sussex Weekly Advertiser* refers to him in glowing terms, on January 24, 1803.

The Gentlemen of Brighton have it in contemplation to erect in that town, a Mill of considerable dimension to be worked from, a plan of which is preparing by Mr. Pilbeam, whose professional fame has been widely extended by the superiority of the structure of our town mill and the integrity of which he performed his contract with the Subscribers.

The document – Subscribers to the Lewes Public Corn Mill – lists the sixty-

SUBSCRIBERS TO THE PUBLIC CORN MILL

Abergavenny, the Earl of
Attwood, William
Blackman, Sir Henry
Baker, John
Boys, John Esq
Blair, Dr MD
Blaker, John
Campion, William Esq
Chichester, the Earl of
Chatfield, John
Comber, Benj Esq
Chitty, C
Cater, John
Clitherow, James Esq
Courthope, the Rev Wm
Cooper, William Esq
Crockford, William
Fuller, John Esq MP
Goldsmith, Joseph
Gwynne, the Rev William
Hick, WF
Hook, Mary (the late Charles Gilbert)
Hudson, Thomas
Hoper, John Esq
Jackson, Henry Esq
Johnstone, Thomas
Kell, Christopher
Kemp, Thomas Esq
King, Richard
Langridge, WB (the late)
Lemperiere, Amon
Rockford, William
Chase, Richard Esq

Diggens, James
Dunstone, Samuel
Dunn, Robert
Fisher, John
Lee, William
Lee, Arthur
Molineux, Joseph
Madgwick, William
Neal, Robert
Pelham, the Rt Hon Lord
Pelham, JC Esq
Payne, Trayton
Poole, Sir Ferdinando
Partington, Thomas Esq
Raymond, VA
Rand, Charles Esq
Read, Thomas
Raynes, the Rev ER
Rideout, the Rev
Shelly, Henry Esq
Snashall, Samuel
Smith, Josias Esq
Shadwell, H Esq
Shelley, Henry Jun
Standby, Thomas
Tourle, Thomas Esq
Whiteman, John
Wille, Charles
Whitefield, Francis Esq
Wille, George
Wild, Amon
Willard, Fredk

five subscribers, all men (apart from Mary Hook, who donated money on behalf of the late Charles Gilbert). The money was collected in three or four instalments, the first being 25 per cent, the second, 50 per cent and the third 25 per cent, making up the total of £10 from each. The fourth subscription was for a further £5, paid by thirty-five of the subscribers. Of this, fifteen payments of £5 were paid to Joseph Goldsmith, builder. William Cooper paid his £5 for the provision of a fence; two payments were paid to William Lee; twelve were paid directly to the bank, on April 20 and 30; the rest were paid by personal bills. Presumably, the fourth subscription amounting to £175, was to pay for the construction of the round house and £650 was the cost of the mill.

The lease on the mill was to commence at Michaelmas, 1801, for a term of ninety-nine years, at a yearly rent of £3.3s. The lease laid down the stringent rules and regulations pertaining to the use of the area. The tenants had the right to use a new footway or passage leading from the mill to the High Street, through the rest of the croft and through other property of the Earl of Chichester and Thomas, Lord Pelham, occupied by William Smith and Henry Waller. The Earl reserved a right of way, for the tenants of the property occupied by William Smith, to go through the plot from Castle Banks to the rest of the plot, and to take carriages and beasts that were to be slaughtered to the stable, pound and slaughterhouse. There was a right of footway only from the remainder of the plot to the High Street. The tenants of the property occupied by Henry Waller had a similar right of footway, with permission to carry timber and other materials from the High Street into their workshops.

The committee covenanted to repair the gates and fences, provide ironwork for the waingates of the two pieces of land and hinges and a lock and a bolt for the gate at the northern end of the passage. The Earl and his tenant, Henry Waller, reserved the right to lock the gate at the High Street end of the passage and at the north end, at ten in the evening until four in the morning. All committee members and their servants were to have keys. In the event of the removal of the windmill, the committee was to reinstate the land at members' own cost, making it fit for tillage and as even as possible. The land was said to be 'somewhat on a declivity from west to east'.

However hard the subscribers and the committee worked to get the mill up and running there was still anxiety that it was not going to be quick enough. The fear of local insurrection in the town and the surrounding areas was overshadowed by the pressing fear of a French invasion by Napoleon. In 1801 the government hastily implemented a new Act, Defence and Security of the Realm During the Present War.

A meeting called at the White Hart, Lewes on August 13, 1801, resolved:

That it is the most anxious wish of this meeting, zealously and cordially, either in their public or private capacities, to co-operate as far as they are able with such arrangements as His Majesty shall in his Wisdom think proper to direct for carrying into Execution the provisions of the Act of Parliament . . . or for otherwise providing for the Defence of the Kingdom in which this County having nearly ninety miles of Coast immediately opposite to and within twelve hours Sail of the Enemy feels itself most deeply and particularly interested.

On September 14, a meeting was held at the Star Inn to consider fully the implications of the new Act. It authorised the Lieutenancy and the Quarter Sessions to prepare contingency plans to be instigated in the event of an invasion. The schedules were extremely detailed, preparing the town for every eventuality and today, make fascinating reading.

Schedule 2 lists the parishes in the

Rape of Lewes and details the amount of livestock, riding horses, waggons, carts, other carriages, draft horses and oxen. It lists the number of bridges in each parish and the number of boats and barges that could be brought into use. Corn mills, both wind and water, were enumerated and the proposed quantity of corn which could be ground in twenty-four hours. Ovens, both private and in bakeries, were listed. St Michael's parish had four bakeries and three private ovens at its disposal and could produce 12,740 loaves of bread daily.

Schedule 7 of the Act required the Commissioners of the Public Town Mill, John Whiteman, Joseph Goldsmith, and William Lee, to supply five sacks of flour weighing 280 pounds, every twenty-four hours, The schedule noted that there was no wheat or cloth available at the mill and this would have to be provided from another source.

Schedule 9 tells us that William Smart would provide between 600 and 800 loaves daily.

Fortunately for the country, the county, the town and, not least, the mill committee the French invasion did not take place, as the Town Mill was not in operation until the following year.

At last, some good news for the people of Lewes, when a further announcement was placed in the *Advertiser* on February I, 1802:

MILLERS WANTED. A grinder in every respect to conduct the business of the PUBLIC WIND MILL, lately erected within the BOROUGH OF LEWES. Persons of the above description, who are desirous of undertaking the same are requested to give their attendance at a General Meeting of the Subscribers to be holden at the STAR INN, LEWES, on Tuesday the ninth of February instant, at eleven o'clock in the forenoon. By order of the Committee, LANGRIDGE and KELL Secretaries.

And:

The public windmill erected for similar purposes in this Borough under the direction of Mr. Pilbeam, it is expected, will be in a state to grind in the course of a fortnight.

The mill was indeed in working order by February 22, when further newspaper reports tell us:

. . . Its operations, both on wheat and barley, exceeded the most sanguine expectations of the proprietors.

The townspeople were informed that the mill would be for grinding corn at a reasonable price and that employers using the mill could expect the grinding to be done fairly. The scale of charges would be fourpence a bushel for wheat, threepence a bushel for hog corn.

With all obstacles overcome the committee was able to turn its attention to celebrations to mark the opening of the mill. It was decided to hold a Grand Concert and Ball to encourage the gentry to continue their interest in the mill and to support the poor financially.

The ball was deemed a great success and a report in the *Sussex Weekly Advertiser*, on March 1, records:

The concert and ball in honour of the above mill, on Thursday, met the sanctions and support of all the fashionable families in the town and neighbourhood, and we believe, of

19

all military gentleman stationed here, whose distinguished attendance on the occasion, could be viewed in no other light than as a handsome compliment paid to the town, which was rendered the more conspicuous by the complacency that accompanied it. The dancing commenced at ten and concluded with the DUSTY MILLER about one in the morning.

What a sparkling evening that must have been. The report has all the flavour of a Jane Austen novel. It has been rumoured that she visited Lewes at about this time and her unfinished novel, *The Watsons*, starts with an account of such a ball. Perhaps, just perhaps, Miss Austen may have honoured the mill committee with her presence.

LEWES
PUBLIC WIND CORN MILL

On Thursday next, the 25th of February, 1802
THERE WILL BE
A Grand Concert and Ball.
At the STAR INN LEWES
For the BENEFIT of the industrious POOR;
*Under the Direction of the Committee appointed
to erect the Mill.*
☞ The Performance will begin at Seven o'clock
precisely.

The Committee wish it to be understood, that the purchasers of tickets, will be entitled to dispose of proportionate part of the money received after paying the necessary expences,—to be delivered in flour, from the mill, to those to whom they have given the tickets, after having presented them for their admission at the door. They therefore request, that such Ladies and Gentlemen, as intend honouring the Concert with their support, will make an early application for them to Mr. DUNN, at the Star Inn, who has received directions to issue a limited number, only, to prevent any inconvenience taking place from too large an assemblage.

The Committee feel great pleasure in returning their thanks to the Gentlemen of the Sussex Regiment, who offered their full Band on the present occasion. they flatter themselves, that the inhabitants of and its neighbourhood, will, by a numerous attendance, give, that sanction which they conceive they some reason to expect, on the completion of so distinguished and beneficial a work

Tickets, 3s. 6d. each.
CHAISES, AS USUAL.

The mill was working for less than two years when disaster befell it on Wednesday, December 28, 1803. A violent storm lashed the town causing severe damage. The local paper reported that two of the mill's swifts were blown off during the gale. No doubt the millwright and his labourers would have set to work to restore the mill to working order as soon as the weather improved.

At the beginning of 1804 the country was still in a state of emergency with fears of French invasion ever present. The Constables, on inspecting bread for sale, found again that some of it was short in weight. Further investigations were made and it was discovered that certain bakers, who sold their bread at a discount to other retailers, were guilty of giving short weight – but craftily not in their own premises. Those bakers found to have committed this crime were charged a hefty five shillings an ounce fine.

At the same time, there was growing concern in the town that the mill committee was in some kind of financial difficulty. It was reported that the committee had failed to pay the Poor Tax to the Overseers of St Michael's parish. It was resolved unanimously by the vestry members, that if the committee continued to be in default, members would be sued for the money owing. A further note, written in the same week announced that the mill would now be taxed at £5 per annum.

Things were to get worse. The Reverend Harry West, curate of St Michael's church, resigned on April 29 after thirteen years' ministry. He stated that in recent years he had received no tithes or Easter offerings from the Committee of the Wind Corn Mill, in lieu of a regular stipend for his services. He went as far as to place a memorandum to this effect in the parish register.

. . . but receiving no tithe from the Corn Mill by defalcation of revenues by Subscribers to the Mill . . . and that no exemption can be pleaded on the score of Custom by the aforesaid subscribers in the St. Michael's Parish.

Defalcate means to misuse or misappropriate property or funds. In other words – trouble at t'mill! In *Recollections of a Sussex Parson*, Boys Ellman describes West as an 'extraordinary character . . . very quarrelsome'. He was, apparently, a man of the cloth who appeared to be somewhat lacking in Christian charity. As a minister he did nothing to support Boys Ellman when he was a young curate at Berwick. He tried his best to lower Ellman's stipend from £40 a year, and when this tactic failed, West tried to make Ellman responsible for paying the rates on the rectory. West then demanded £5 for a clock that should have been in the house by right, and when Ellman refused to pay, West sent his carriage and watchmaker to collect it.

Extensive research has failed to find further reference to the defalcation and no evidence can be found to suggest that the committee was taken to task for misdeeds, other than that it was forced, by law, to place the mill up for sale. An advertisement was placed in the *Sussex Weekly Advertiser* on October 7, 1805:

Lewes. To be disposed of, A good well-timbered Windmill with two pairs of stones, a machine and bolting mill complete. To be removed from the present situation which is in the neighbourhood of Lewes. Apply for a reference to Mr. Arthur Lee.'

Lewes Windmill.

TO BE

Sold by Auction,

BY VERRALL AND SON,

AT THE STAR INN, LEWES,

On SATURDAY, the 27th Day of JUNE, instant,

AT SIX O'CLOCK IN THE AFTERNOON,

Subject to such Conditions as will then be produced.

A VALUABLE

Wind Corn Mill,

WITH THE

LEASE OF THE GROUND AND PREMISES,

Thereto belonging, granted for ninety-nine years, at the low rent of Three Guineas, of which Term eighty-eight years will be unexpired at Michaelmas next.

The MILL is situate in the Parish of St. Michael's, in Lewes, adjacent to, and communicating nearly at the centre with the High-street; was built by Pilbean, of the very best materials, has been since used as a Public Town-Mill, and is one of the most complete buildings of that class. Immediate possession may be had.

The interior of the Mill may be viewed, and the stipulations of the Lease examined, by applying at the Office of Messrs. Langridge and Kell, Solicitors, Lewes.

Lewes: 13 June, 1812.

LEWES PRINTED BY W. AND A. LEE

Advertisement in The Sussex Weekly Advertiser, June 12, 1812.

The mill was not sold. As a result the original committee of Henry Jackson, William Hick, William Lee, Joseph Goldsmith, and the acting committee of Thomas Blair, the Reverend Edward Raynes, Samuel Dunstone, Frederick Williard and John Bannister, were forced to take out a mortgage on the mill for £420 from William Campion and the Reverend ER Raynes. An interest debt of £105 had already accrued on it. A further attempt to sell the lease was made in 1808.

22

TO MILLERS
TO BE SOLD BY PRIVATE CONTRACT
A large good timbered SMOCK
WINDMILL, erected but a few years since.
For further particulars apply to Mr. Lee,
printer, Lewes, if by letter postage paid.

Again, the mill remained unsold. Following the death of Thomas Pelham at Stanmer on June 18, 1805, the freehold of his many properties were put up for sale. On the June 6 and 7, 1810, the Town Corn Mill and other Pelham property including stable, carpenters' shops and slaughterhouses, were sold by Ann, the Dowager Countess of Chichester, her son, Thomas, the new Earl, and Thomas Partington, a trustee of Pelham's will, to Robert Neal, cordwainer, of Lewes and his trustee, Thomas King, for £1,120.

A third attempt to dispose of the lease of the mill was made in 1812. This time, not by a private sale, but by auction.

As a result, on January 14, 1813, the committee and the mortgage-holders sold the lease of the mill and other buildings, plus fixtures and utensils, for the outstanding sum of £525, to James Lade the younger, a miller.

It is worth noting here that one of the committee members, Joseph Goldsmith, the builder, had been declared bankrupt. Was he the culprit?

To bring this important part of the mill's history to an end, one can positively conclude that the Public Subscription Wind Corn Mill gave loyal service to those in desperate need and may even have played its part in preventing what might well have been insurrection and food riots on the streets of Lewes.

The second phase of the mill's history, on its original site, was somewhat brief and little is known of the new owner, James Lade, other than that he a was a miller, living in Lewes. Having bought the mill, he worked it for just over a year, but then decided to move to Chiddingly. He put the mill back on the market and sold it to William Smart, corn chandler, on April 6, 1814, for £700, making a substantial profit. One is left wondering why William Smart failed to purchase the mill from the mill committee when it was first put up for sale.

THREE

HOW DOES A SMOCK MILL WORK?

Solemn sentinel, lone and still
Watchful, weather-worn, wise old mill
Have you a quaint philosophy
Won through years of adversity?

GM Powell

Having considered why the mill was built it would be helpful now to examine how and why it was built as a smock mill. Looking at the evidence, we have the original specifications set out by the committee, and the advertisement details used when the mill was finally sold in 1812. There is some pictorial evidence and two contemporary map references. William Figg's map of 1799 shows the Town Mill already in position, although construction did not start until 1801. James Edward's map of 1817 shows the windmill clearly marked. William Lambert's engraving, published by J Baxter, in 1816,

The Iconography of Lewes,
James Edwards 1799

shows a cricket match being played on the Paddock. On the horizon the Town Mill is clearly visible. A painting of Lewes from the Combe, by Gideon Mantell in 1813, also shows a small image of the mill.

A photograph *c*1870 shows the original smock tower of the mill in its new location on Race Hill, with Lewes Prison in the background.

Let us look at the exterior first. Maybe, because there was a cost limit and the fact that timber was cheap and readily available, the smock design was chosen as the most suitable in contrast to the more permanent brick tower mills, which were their contemporaries.

The name smock was used because of the supposed resemblance of the outline of the building to the smock worn by the working countrymen of the day. The mill was a conventional eight-sided, tapering wooden tower with overlapping weatherboarding. The framework consisted of eight cant or corner posts with diagonal struts for rigidity, over

The mill is on the skyline of this Lambert engraving of cricket on the Paddock.

which the boarding was laid horizontally and the corners sealed with pitch or, in other cases, with lead or zinc strips to prevent water penetration and subsequent rotting of the timber.

This heavy framework surmounted the two-storey hexagonal base built of flint and brick, which is the round house.

The patterning of bricks and flints on the upper part of The Round House.

It was built with two high entrances to the front and rear to allow easy access for carts to the ground floor where grain would have arrived and flour been despatched. The base served as a strong foundation for the smock, and protected it from rain-water erosion.

Undoubtedly vital machinery would have been housed within the stout walls. Bearing in mind that the mill was built to a budget, the external design of the upper part of the round house was thoughtful; the flints and bricks were mapped out in a symmetrical, repeating pattern. A treble row of bricks was laid with ends protruding, encircling the eight sides of the building. The majority of the bricks in the middle row are shored off now, suggesting that they had a utilitarian purpose other than being decorative; may be they underpinned a roofing stage, which gave the miller access to his sweeps.

The lower part of the round house walls were built rather haphazardly, with no time wasted on decorative construction. This could suggest that this part of the house was less visible and did not warrant such attention to detail.

The round house was built with sliding sash windows and the window cills rest on red quarry tiles. Windows in the smock would have required the miller to keep a close eye on ensuring that this area remained waterproof. There were four wooden sails, also known as sweeps or swifts, and these were likely fitted with the double spring shutters that had come into use in 1772. The shutters opened and shut as the sweeps revolved, to catch and spill the wind. They were a great improvement on the earlier method of reefing and rearranging large sheets of canvas over the open sweep of bays.

A later photograph of the smock shows that crowning the top of the wooden tower was the domed copper cap through which emerged the windshaft – to which the sweeps were attached. Within the cap was the brake wheel and around this wheel was the brake band which was applied to stop the smock. It was from this large

A French burr stone.

wheel that the power was transmitted via the long upright shaft and other gearing to turn the grindstones. The essential criteria of keeping the sweeps continually into the eye of the wind was effected by means of an eight-vaned fantail located at the rear of the cap causing it to revolve on a metal kerb at the top of the smock tower.

Tool used for stone dressing.

Like other smock mills, the Town Mill would have had five floors in the smock and the round house. Beneath the cap would have been the bin floor where the grain was stored for grinding. Sacks of grain were lifted up through one-way trap doors on each floor by means of the sack hoist. On the next floor down, the grain fell through sacking or wooden chutes into the hoppers and then into the millstones. Stones called French burrs were used to produce fine flour. They comprised wedges of freshwater churt, arranged in a perfect circle, cemented together and bound with two iron bands.

The grain passed from the hopper into the wooden shoe and was agitated into a hole in the centre to this level through of the upper stone. This stone, known as the runner, rotated above the stationary bed stone beneath. As the grain passed between the two surfaces it was cut, crushed and ground.

The mill operated a boulter which was a cylindrical wooden frame encased in a woollen mesh. The mesh was a fine gauge at the top and grew coarser towards the bottom. The flour was thus graded by its consistency, the fine flour passing out of the boulter first, the

Gideon Mantell's watercolour of Lewes, with the mill seen on the horizon.

coarsest flour and bran at the end. Cooled flour – which had become warm due to the friction between the stones – then passed to the meal floor where it was weighed and bagged and made ready for distribution.

William Figg's Town Map of Lewes

FOUR

THE PEOPLE WHO LIVED AND WORKED IN THE MILL AND THE ROUND HOUSE

In the narrow little Pipe's Passage, nearly opposite the Bull House, is the base of the old town windmill, converted into an amusing little dwelling house.

Esther Meynell

As William Smart and his extended family played a major role in the history of the Town Mill, Smart's Mill and Shelley's Mill as it later became, and the Round House, it seems appropriate to give some time to a detailed history of the people who lived and worked in these buildings.

Since we are dealing with a period from 1814 to the end of the nineteenth century, this span will be broken down into the context of the families who shared the time. First, we will look at the Smarts, William and his son Samuel Hyde (sometimes Hide), followed by the Shelleys, the family that William's daughter, Elizabeth, married into. Finally we follow the lives of three of Joseph and Elizabeth Shelley's sons who went on to make a significant impact on the town. Passing references will be made to other members of this large family and those who played a significant role in the affairs of the church, local government and the social welfare of Lewes.

I have chosen to give not purely an historic account but also to reflect on sociological and psychological influences on the family. I have discovered snippets of their lives in parish registers, newspapers, censuses, guardian minute books, the International Genealogical Index, graveyard memorials, local authority reports and wills.

Each little piece of new information has been greeted with great excitement as it helped to fill in the intriguing missing bits in the family jigsaw. I have used a chronological framework to present the history of the family and have given a little local and national background history to place them in the social context of the time.

Working on the family history, I was aware that my research was almost completely about men and, as a feminist, this troubled me. I knew that the role of many women of this period was almost overlooked and unrecorded as they toiled away as daughters, wives, spinsters, mothers and grandmothers, having little or no influence in the public domain. Things were beginning to change and gradually women were gaining some freedom to pursue work outside the home. Unmarried women of the middle and lower middle classes found work as governesses and companions. Working class women gravitated to the newly-opened factories, or into service, relieving the upper classes of household chores and care of their children and allowing them to enjoy painting, needlepoint, writing journals and playing music.

So wherever possible I have drawn the women of these families into the picture and described as much of their lives as I could discern from the limited material available to me.

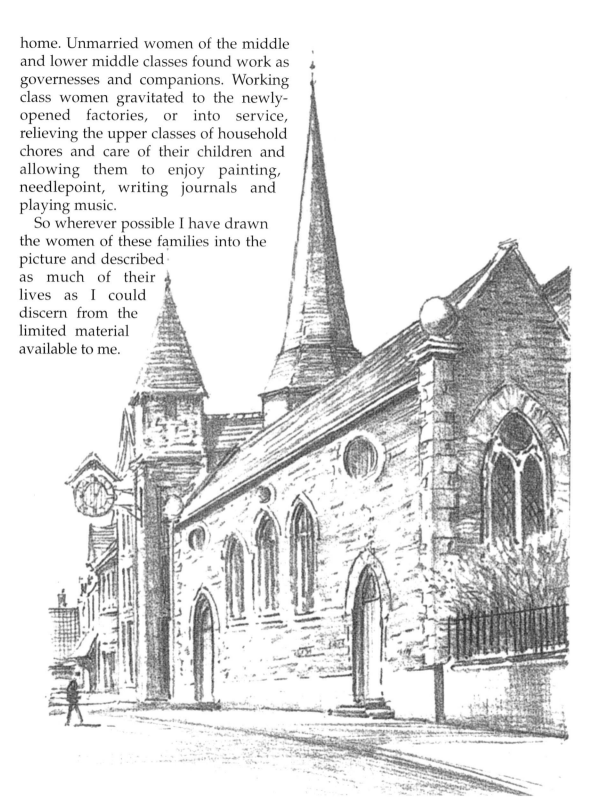

St Michael in Lewes where the Smart family worshipped.

29

FIVE

WILLIAM SMART 1772-1837
FRANCES HYDE 1762-1849

Still following the windings when they slope upwards and after broading out for a space, narrow again, one comes upon a characteristic bit of very ancient track. On the right is the hexagonal structure of a windmill, which has lately been turned into a charming place of residence, without the smallest disturbance of its exterior.

F Frankfort Moore

William Smart was born in 1772, to Thomas and Sarah Smart, living in St Michael's parish. Little is known of his life until he reached his majority and married Frances Hyde (also spelled Hide), a spinster, somewhat older, aged thirty. Their marriage took place on November 3, 1793, at St Michael's, with Curate West officiating. Frances was the daughter of John and Elizabeth Hyde, née Bennett, of the same parish. *The Poll Book* of 1768 gives Thomas Smart's trade as labourer, but by 1790 he had upgraded his skills and was working as a coachman. It is not recorded but there is reason to believe that he was working for John Shelley, carrier. John Hyde, Frances' father, trading as a baker, was involved in the local political scene and held the position of Headborough in 1772. After John Hyde's death in 1776, his widow,

Parish register entry of the marriage of William Smart and Frances Hide.

Elizabeth, continued working the bakery at 75 High Street.

William Bennett, Frances' grandfather, was a witness at her wedding to William Smart. He worked as a tailor in a family business that supplied the gentry. In 1741 he was chosen as Headborough and in 1755 and 1770, a Junior Constable. In 1787 he took up the senior position as Constable of the town. In 1805 he was one of the founder members of a circulating library in the Cliffe, Lewes.

Frances Smart bore her husband three children, Elizabeth, born April 5, 1795, Frances, born May 21, 1797 and Samuel Hyde, born July 18, 1799. Frances, the daughter, died shortly after Samuel was born, and her burial is recorded in the parish registers in November 1799. A small stone in St Michael's churchyard reads: '*In memory of Frances Smart died 28th November 1799 aged 2 years 7 months*'.

William Smart was listed in *Bailey's Universal Directory* as a baker, in 1794, having taken over his mother-in-law's business. *The Poll Book* of 1796 records him as a freeholder, owning two properties in St Martin's Lane and voting in favour of Thomas Kemp and John Cresset Pelham, the Liberal candidates.

The Smarts were devout Anglicans. They had their children baptised at St Michael's and laid their loved ones to rest in the beautiful churchyard. The 1803 *List of the Seatholders of St Michael's Church* records two references for William Smart; one for 4 St Martins Lane (listed as Smart's Cow House) the other, 'William Smart and family living at 74 High Street, Lewes and occupying pew 9 in the Church'.

Walking into the church today, and looking down towards the altar, one can imagine William and Fanny and their

St Martin's Lane, where the Smart family owned property.

two young children, ensconced in their family pew, listening solemnly to the sermon delivered by the Reverend George Proctor.

The family lived out their religious beliefs by contributing to the care of the less fortunate in the parish. At this date the poor were the responsibility of the parish and were dependent on individual acts of charity and on the Poor Rate, which was levied on the richer parishioners. These monies gave some financial and material help to the deserving poor, widows, orphans, the sick and the elderly. In March 1799, the overseers and the churchwardens of St Michael's parish agreed that a rate would be set at three shillings and sixpence in the pound. William Smart, listed as a householder with outbuildings, contributed 13s 1d to the fund. He continued making these quarterly donations up until 1806, when a parish memorandum declared that this method of collecting poor relief was both unsatisfactory and unfair and should be stopped.

In 1801, when contingency plans were drawn up because of the fear of French invasion, William Smart was listed as one of four bakers who would supply 12,740 loaves of bread in twenty-four hours for the people of St Michael's parish.

William had grown up in a family with strong interests in serving the town, and had married into another one. So it was not surprising that he entered local politics in 1802, when chosen – at the Court Leet – to be a Headborough.

Here it may be helpful to include a brief outline of how local government was organised at this date. The roots of local government in Lewes originated from the Merchant Guild of Saxon times, where already there were rules and regulations regarding law and order, taxation for local purposes and a protection of trading practices that worked in favour of those in the Merchant Guild.

This form of government began to fall away during the twelfth and thirteenth centuries, to be replaced by a Society of Twelve, whose members were drawn from 'the wealthier and discreeter sort of townsmen'. Each October two High Constables and two Headboroughs were elected for a one-year period. At the same meeting, held on Whit Monday, the outgoing Constables presented their accounts for their year. Lesser officers (Bailiff, Pound Keeper, Town Crier, Clerk of the Butchery, Clerk to the Fishery, Clerk of the Hostelry, the Ale Conner, Bell Ringer, Searcher of the Leather and the three-man night watch) were also elected at this time.

The Constables had a variety of responsibilities, including that of maintaining law and order by apprehending criminals and vagabonds and maintaining methods of punishment and imprisonment. They inspected ale houses and gaming rooms, maintained roads and bridges, ran the markets, checked weights and measures, cared for the poor and supervised the settlement or removal of itinerants and beggars.

In February, 1808, William was called up for enlistment to the militia. His engagement in war work as a baker gave him the right to submit a substitute to go to the line in his place, and John Terry was the man chosen.

The Sussex Militia Society was an organisation formed for those men who wished to insure themselves against the cost of hiring substitutes to take their places. Those who wanted to take this course of action were assured, by the society, that they could do so on 'liberal terms'.

In 1809 William Smart was elected a Junior Constable. His role was to act as go-between for the lesser officers and the High Constable, and to liaise with the Quarter Session. Both Constables and Headboroughs carried the Staff of Office. For the Constables this was a silver-topped wooden truncheon, about a foot long with the arms of the borough painted on it. A Constable's year of office was commemorated with his name engraved on a silver plaque attached to the stave. The Headboroughs' stave was much longer, measuring five foot six inches, and on the base was a double brass cone and pike. The top held a silver cap engraved with the name of the Headborough. The names of previous Headboroughs were engraved on silver, brass or copper plates attached to the stave. This regalia, although no longer in use, may be viewed in Lewes Town Hall.

The 1811 *St Michael's Population List* shows another move for the family. William Smart was listed at 4 St Martin's Lane with his wife, daughter Elizabeth and son, Samuel Hyde. The hand-written book *The Occupiers and Proprietors of the Houses in Lewes in 1812* (assembled when Lewes houses were numbered) reveals a move from St Martin's Lane to 3 Market Street, to a house belonging to Lord Hampden. The accuracy of this record seems questionable. In John Houghton's list, the family was still occupying 75 High Street. William also owned 4 and 5 St Martin's Lane, occupied by Henry Ford and Mrs Drawbridge.

In 1814 William Smart bought the lease on the Town Mill, from James Lade, miller of Chiddingly, for £700 'of lawful British money'. The measurement of the parcel of land, according to the deeds, was said to be 'thirty–five square roods and one quarter'.

The Poll Book of 1814 gives William' s trade as corn chandler, overseeing the

work at the Town Mill. Mill work was arduous and hazardous and many accidents occurred. The space inside the mill was confined, the machinery heavy and young lads were left to operate it, often with dire consequences. The *Sussex Weekly Advertiser* of 1817 reports:

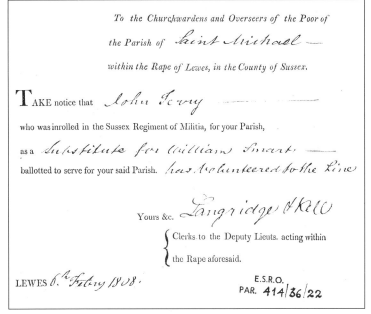

The substitution certificate allowing John Terry to serve in the Sussex Regiment of Militia in place of William Smart.

On Monday last, a lad about 14 years old, son of Mr Smart, Miller, Lewes, in shifting the wheat stones of his father's mill without dropping the break, had one of his hands drawn into the cog wheel and suffered a fracture of several of his fingers, but a cure is thought will be affected without amputation.

In his *Journal*, Gideon Mantell records other mill accidents where he, as a doctor, was asked to attend. The first was at Malling Mill, on November 5, 1821, when a boy had his finger so severely cut that his forefinger and thumb needed to be amputated. The second, which was far more serious, happened at Chailey

Mill ten days later when a young lad got his clothes entangled with the machinery while the windmill was working. As a result of his dreadful injuries the boy died an agonizing death.

In October 1818 William Smart was elected High Constable. *The Town Book of Lewes* records a busy year. On more mundane matters it was resolved that a shop under the Market Tower should be let for a rent of eight guineas to John Duplock, a butcher. The Constables and Headborough, and some members of the Jury, were to walk the boundaries of Godfrey's land and consider the state of the timber growing there. A decision to provide a new Engine House, to accommodate the town's fire fighting equipment and a Record Room had been made in September 1817. A site had been purchased on the east side of Fisher Street and Amon Wild, the architect, had been instructed to draw up plans for the building. Although the sum of £20 had been deducted from the Constables' accounts towards the costs, it was necessary to raise further money by public subscription to pay for the works. One hundred and twenty-two people raised the required capital of £138 1s 6d, and a further eight people paid for the fire insurance. William Smart donated a guinea, as did Mrs John Shelley, who was shortly to become an in-law.

At that time, the role of women remained very much in the shadows and there was little acknowledgement of their role in society, other than as wife and mother. So it was with great delight that I found information on the Female Philanthropic Society in a catalogue of examples, printed by Baxter of Lewes in 1818. The society was not radical in its aspirations, barely challenging the stereotypical role of women, but it was interesting to see that a small group of women had initiated the society without the patronage of men. The society acted as an outward manifestation of these women's Christian beliefs 'inasmuch as ye have done it unto one of the least of these, ye have done it unto me'.

The society provided linen for the children of the poor, and warm clothing for the elderly and the destitute. The list of subscribers included Mrs John Shelley, who donated £1, which entitled her to become a director, and Mrs William Smart, who gave the more reserved four shillings that allowed her to nominate three people to 'partake of its benefits'.

A matter of great importance in the town was the Parliamentary election to return two members to represent the Borough of Lewes. As Constables, it was the responsibility of William Smart and Thomas Whiteman to officiate at the election, which began on June 15, 1818, and continued to the following day. The borough was much smaller than it is today and comprised the four parishes of St Anne, St John-sub-Castro, St Michael and All Saints.

Prior elections in 1812 and 1816 were smeared with rumours of bribery and corruption. As a result of these serious accusations, it was noted in the Court Leet volume of 1817-1818 that the Act Against Bribery and Corruption was read in the open court as a reminder to all. One presumes that Smart and Whiteman were extremely vigilant that these offences would not occur while the election was run under their control.

A note written on the front page of *The Poll Book*, in William Smart's hand, states:

Borough } to wit   A Poll taken by William Smart and
of Lewes   Thomas Whitman Constables of the said
Borough on the fifteenth day of June
and continued by adjournment to the following Day
1818, for the Election of two Burgesses
to represent the said Borough in the Parliament summoned
to be holden at Westminster on the 4th day of August next

Candidates

George Shiffner Esqr. nominated by Josias Smith Esqr.
and seconded by John Chatfield Esqr.

Sir John Shelley Bart nominated by John Hoper Esqr.
and seconded by Thomas Rogers Esqr —

The Honble Thos Erskine nominated by Henry Blackman Esqr.
and seconded by Ebenezer Johnston Esqr. —

_____

NB. The Letter S stands for Shiffner. the Letters Sh. for
Shelley. and the Letter E for Erskine. and the
strokes under those Letters the Candidates for whom the Electors
polled —

On the second day of Election Henry Baring Esq was nominated
by Mr Wm Elphick and seconded by Mr Tugwell
and his Qualification was demanded by two Electors Mr Michell
Trisk and Mr Frederick Boore but Mr Baring not being present the
votes in the fourth Column marked under the token S were taken for Mr Baring

Inside page of the 1818 Poll Book showing William Smart's handwritten comment.

35

A Poll taken by William Smart and Thomas Whiteman Constables of the said Borough on the fifteenth day of June 1818 . . and continued by adjournment to the following day for the Election of two Burgesses to represent the said Borough in the Parliament to be holden at Westminister on the 4th day of August.

On the bottom of the page was:

On the second day of (the) Election Henry Baring Esq. was nominated by Mr. Wm. Elphick and seconded by Mr. Tugwell and his qualification was demanded by two electors, by Mr. Michael Irish and Mr. Frederick Boore, but Mr. Baring not being present, the votes in the fourth column marked under the letter B was taken for Mr. Baring.

A vote of thanks on behalf of the two elected was published on June 17, 1815:

We have hitherto endeavoured to discharge our Duty in Parliament, according to the honest and sincere opinions which we severally entertained of it, and we will persevere in acting on the same principle.'

The Town Book of Lewes records that:

'The thanks of the meeting were unanimously voted to the Constables for their impartial Conduct in the Business of the day upon the motion of Sir George Shiffner seconded by Sir John Shelley.'

The Lewes Liberals, including Smart senior and Smart junior, were totally disheartened and disillusioned by the outcome of the election in 1818 and failed to regain their determination to fight for electoral justice, in 1820, when Shelley and Shiffner were returned again, without contest.

On May 20, 1819, Elizabeth Smart, aged twenty-one, married Joseph Shelley of Castle Precincts at St Michael's.

Samuel Hyde Smart worked with his father in the flourishing family business at the Town Mill, which continued on its original site until 1819 when, for some undefined reason, it was decided to remove the smock to a site near to the barracks, where Lewes Prison now stands.

It was thought that the seven new cottages, known as Prospect Row, built to the rear of the mill, affected the wind flow to the sweeps, but the James Edwards map of May, 1817, and the J Marchant survey of 1824 show no houses on the site. The Listed Buildings survey suggests that the houses were built in 1830.

William made the momentous decision to shift the smock, sweeps and the workings of the mill to the new site. William Medhurst, the local millwright, had the unenviable task of removing it. After dismantling the smock it was transferred on a trolley, pulled by bullocks, to the new location. One can only imagine the tremendous difficulties caused by the weight and size of the smock and sweeps, the rough conditions of the terrain over which it was moved, and the logistical problems of manoeuvring the load around corners and uphill to the mill's new situation.

The smock was re-erected on a one-storey brick round house at its new site. When the prison opened in 1853 it was found that this new building interfered with the wind flow and the round house was heightened, without removing the smock. The mill was driven by four double-shuttered sweeps.

Whether the round house in Pipe Passage was converted into a dwelling immediately after the removal of the smock is not known. An early print of unknown date shows that a thatched roof has been added to the round house, and a lean-to built on to the west side, with an entrance and a chimney stack. An internal door was built behind the main rear entrance, probably to make the house warmer and more habitable. In the print, the mill house appears to be unfettered by any other dwellings close by but this may be an artistic impression. A flint wall on the east of the property may be seen, with a gateway to the castle ditch. Artistic licence makes the castle appear much closer than it is in reality. The picket fence affords a boundary and the path leads to the High Street. The millstones used to form a path to the house remain in situ, today.

As a result of new legislation in 1818-1819, a Select Vestry was set up in each parish throughout the country. Those elected to the Select Vestry were required to be substantial house owners or occupiers. At least five members and no more than twenty were to be chosen. Twenty people were elected to the Select Vestry of St Michael's parish, whose remit was to be the care and management of the poor of the parish through the election of churchwardens. The Vestry Committee was also responsible for the financial affairs, the care of its properties, and for collecting in the rates.

William Smart was one of the elected. The Select Vestry meetings were not held in public, were often self-

Rear view of the Round House after removal of the mill.

37

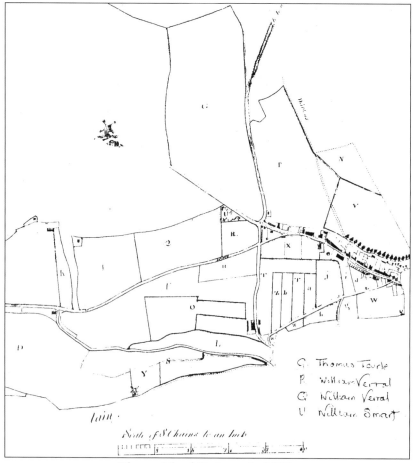

G. Thomas Tourle
P. William Verral
G. William Verral
U. William Smart

The parish of St Anne in 1825.

about 1825, and bordered with land owned by Thomas Tourle and William Verrall.

It is difficult to surmise why William was buying these assorted pieces of land. He was not using it as grazing land and he could not build on it. Perhaps he bought purely for investment purposes.

Although active in acquiring property, running the mill and working as a corn chandler, he maintained an interest in the affairs of the town, was one of the men who fixed the town tax at 6d in the pound on Whit Monday 1821 and he served on the jury in 1823.

In 1828, lists of men, mainly freeholders, were elected to serve as jury members. Both William, working as a corn chandler, and Samuel, as a miller, were nominated to serve as representatives of St Michael's parish.

In 1829 William Smart is recorded as having 'appropriated' pew number nine in the church's refurbished northern gallery.

These box pews were rented by the town worthies, affording them status, and denoted their position in the church and town.

In 1824, William was one of the many subscribers who paid for the publication

perpetuating and therefore open to accusations of corruption.

William's mill on its new site, at Race Hill, was now referred to as Smart's Mill. As well as working as a miller and baker, he had begun to speculate in land purchase. As early as 1803, he had bought a lease on one and a half acres of brook land in Southover, that became known as Smarts' Brook.

In 1823 more brook lands, known as Coombs and Scufflings, near to the Anchor Inn, at Barcombe were purchased, with George Stanford, a Lewes builder. Later these were renamed St Helena. William also held a lease on an acre of land in 'Spittal Lain', shown on a map of of Thomas Horsfield's book *The History of Lewes and its Environs*, printed by John Baxter. He and his family were also members of the Lewes Library Society, founded in 1786, which loaned a wide choice of quality books, both fiction and non-fiction. Membership was by selection. New members were asked for an initial payment of 2s 6d and a monthly subscription of one shilling. By 1802, the library contained 1,342 books and the number continued to rise with increased membership. Works on the sciences, and books, thought to be too expensive for individual purchase, were added for members to borrow from the library.

Magazines were also bought for the library, including *Blackwood's* and the *Sporting Magazine*.

John Button, a Liberal, wrote a long poem in celebration of the Lewes Library Society. The volume was printed with the help of subscription. William Smart, as a library member, was listed as one of the subscribers to the book. From this and from the Smarts' membership of the Library Society, it would seem that they were keen readers.

Elizabeth became a member in 1810, when she was only fifteen. Samuel Smart was admitted to the Library Society on January 9, 1828, in place of Thomas Horsfield, who had been suspended (because he disputed the library committee's decision not to allow the librarian to keep the money raised from fines). On December 5, 1830, at the Star Inn, twenty-two members of the society, including William and Samuel Smart, met to find suitable new premises to accommodate the expanding library. Mr Drakes, owner of the building used by the society, wanted it released and

offered his shop on School Hill in its stead. Mr Dunn, owner of the Star Inn, suggested that a house in Albion Street should be considered. This offer was taken up and the library moved to 3 Albion Street in 1831.

In that same year, William Smart was investing heavily in land. He leased meadowlands from Henry Uridge, in Ringmer, and two years later his son, and George Smith, purchased two parcels of land called Brooke Meadow, adjoining Coombe Brooks. William secured a lease from George Holman, miller, for land and premises, including a windmill, at Rushey Green in Ringmer. This lease was then assigned to Sarah Stanford, the widow of his friend, George Stanford, Charles Wille, timber merchant and John Hilton, builder. Later, the lease passed to Jane Pannet, who carried on the trade as miller until 1856.

April 1831 saw a radical petition signed by 283 householders of Lewes, including William and Samuel Smart, and Joseph Shelley, asking the King to dissolve Parliament on the grounds that it failed to represent the people and 'should represent the Rights of the many, and not the Interests of the few'.

The Lewes petitioners, and others across the kingdom, held that the burden of taxation and the exploitations of the workers were greatly resented. Money was seen to be lavishly wasted by those in power, who did not represent, in any way, the needs of those whom they purported to represent. The petitioners demanded that Parliamentary representation reform should be enforced and with it a reduction in public expenditure on unnecessary fripperies. A further petition was sent to the House of Lords, ' . . . praying their lordships to pass the REFORM BILL'.

The Reform Act was passed in 1832 after a stormy passage through the House of Commons. It brought about changes in the size of parliamentary constituencies. The boundaries of Lewes were now to include the parishes of St Thomas in the Cliffe, South Malling and St John the Baptist, Southover. Castle Precincts continued to remain extra-parochial until 1858. To celebrate the passing of the Reform Act, which had the loyal support of the town, and to encourage people to vote in the forthcoming general election, a procession, led by the Town Crier and the Town Band walked to all the parts of the town now accepted into the constituency. Proclamations and speeches were made and replied to by the Headboroughs and the Constables of the Hundred of Ringmer and Swanborough.

A general election was held on December 10, 1832, and the *East Sussex Poll Book* of 1832 records father and son Smart again casting their votes in favour of the Liberal candidates, Thomas Kemp and Sir Charles Richard Blunt, who were both returned to represent the borough.

In the same year a Royal Commission was set up to examine the old Poor Law. This resulted in the passing of the Poor Law Amendment Act of 1834, which overturned the existing system of the poor being the responsibility of the better off, who were expected to pay a poor rate annually. Under the new Act, local boards of guardians, elected by the ratepayers, were to administer it. Parishes were to be grouped together into poor law unions and each union was to have a workhouse. Three Poor Law commissioners, working in London, and acting through assistant commissioners, were to supervise the incorporation of 13,000 parishes into 573 unions, by 1838.

The implications of the new Act were not well received in Lewes. A meeting was called by Mr M Irish and Stephen Rushbridge, to petition against it as late as March 14, 1838. It is refreshing and reassuring that the ruling people of Lewes had a sense of conscience about the detrimental effects that the new Act would have on the needy, and that they were not averse to voicing them at the highest level in the House of Commons. It was generally felt that the new Act severely penalised those workers and their families living at subsistence level, on a wage often no more than twelve shillings a week. Under the new law there was no real alternative for the family in dire need, other than the workhouse or a life of crime. It often happened that a husband, wife and children were placed in separate workhouses, miles apart, which naturally added to their misery. However, the strongly- worded petition did not prevent the setting up of the first union workhouse, in South Street, Lewes.

Taking a sidewards step to 1834, the Lewes water supply was, in the main, provided by springs and wells, although private water companies did supply the more affluent houses on the High Street. The springs and wells were often unhygienic and polluted by leaking sewage. Outbreaks of cholera, typhus, typhoid and diphtheria were prevalent, hygiene was lax and death a ready visitor to many homes (occupiers of the Mill House drew their water from a well situated to the east of the house).

The Lewes Water Works Company was set up by local plumber William Davey, 'with the purpose of supplying the town of Lewes with pure spring water at a moderate fee per annum'. Shares in the enterprise, at the astronomical price of £25 each, were offered. William Smart, a friend of Davey, realised that there was money to be made in this investment so he, his son, Samuel and son-in-law, Joseph Shelley, all bought into the scheme, paying for their shares in six instalments.

Between 1834 and 1837 William Smart was Clerk to the Market. At that time the town market was held fortnightly on the High Street, outside the Market Tower. A mixed range of goods was offered for sale, including livestock, which would have required Smart to be ever-watchful for malpractice in short weights and unwholesome goods. Samuel Smart became Clerk to the Market from 1853 to 1857 and William's grandson, Joseph Shelley, was to become Clerk to the Fishery between 1862 and 1874.

The last reference to William Smart in the *Lewes Town Book* was made in May 1837, when he was a signatory on the audits for the previous year's spending by the Constables. Two months later, on July 14 – just a few weeks after the start of Victoria's long reign he died, at 6.30am, from 'water on the chest'.

Stone showing the site of the old well at the Round House.

The *Sussex Weekly Advertiser* carried a notice of his death:

Died at Lewes on Friday last, Mr William Smart an old and respected inhabitant, aged 66.

William's son, Samuel, and Isaiah Weller, a butcher from Southover, were executors of the will, which gives an insight into William's considerable estate, and reflects his standing in the town. He left all his properties, including rents and interests, to his wife, Frances, and on her death these would go to his son, Samuel, and daughter, Elizabeth. The properties included his two freehold houses, stable yards and premises in the parish of St Michael (occupied by William King, Harry Reeves and Samuel Smart); a freehold house, garden and premises in the parish of All Saints; a freehold warehouse, cowstall, yard and premises in the parish of St John-sub-Castro (occupied by James Alderton); and the Mill House, in the occupation of Joseph Shelley and William Smart.

The will hints that William had some serious problems in his relationship with his son-in-law, Joseph Shelley. It tied up his properties and monies so that on the death of his wife, Frances, the money due to his daughter, Elizabeth, would go directly to her 'into her own hands for her sole and separate use and Benefit independently and exclusively and without being subject to the Debts or control of the said Joseph Shelley or any future Husband'.

This seemingly contravenes the law that a woman gave up her rights to own property and goods on her marriage and what was hers became her husband's. William Smart clearly did not wish this to happen in respect of his daughter. Joseph Shelley was to receive just five shillings a week, but only at the discretion of the trustees. On the death of

Elizabeth, all the properties left to her were to be sold by auction or private contract and the money raised was to be used to buy stocks and funds in Parliamentary Securities in Great Britain. Her monies, stocks, funds etc were to be divided into equal parts and given to her children. Her sons were to receive their share at the age of twenty-three and the daughters at twenty-one or on marriage. Money was to be made available for the children's education. William's grandsons were to be given money to pay for training in business or a profession. For his granddaughters, money was to be made available for their 'marriage portions'.

Joseph Shelley was to be released from interest that would have accrued on the £25 loan, given to him by William to buy a share in the Lewes Water Works. However, it was further stipulated that if he had sold the share the loan was to be repaid with interest.

Among other lands and properties

that were to be left to his wife, Fran— and on her demise to his son, Sam— were the freehold wind corn m— stables, fields and premises in the par— of St Anne; three dwellings in the par— of St Michael (occupied by Geo— Bailey, baker, his son Samuel Hy— Smart and himself); a parcel — meadowlands and premises in the par— of St John the Baptist, Southover (in — occupation of Henry Brazier, blacksmi— twelve acres of land, a messuage a— gardens, situated in Barcombe, occup— by James Funnell); his house, garden a— field situated in the parish of Horsh— (in the occupation of Messrs We— and Cheeseman).

A special arrangement was made — respect to the windmill. On the death — Frances this was to be sold to Sam— Smart for the sum of £800, either paid — a lump sum or by yearly instalme— of not less the £100. Interest was to be — £5 per annum, paid half yearly. T— capital sum plus interest was to be giv—

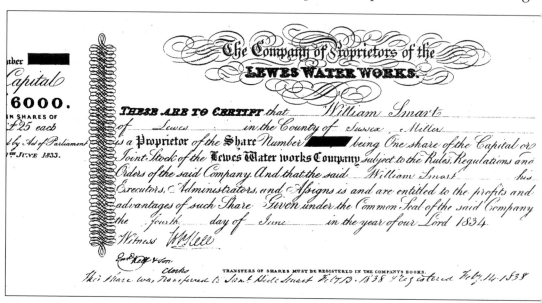

William Smart's Lewes Water Works share certificate.

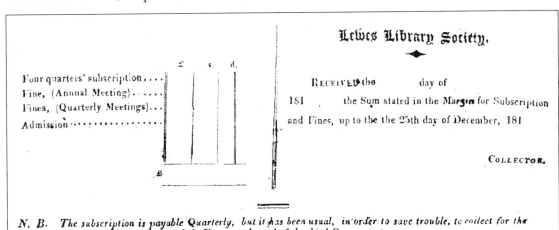

An excerpt from William Smart's will.

to his daughter, Elizabeth.

Then followed a list of personal bequests. To his son, his mahogany desk; his watch seal and chain to his grandson, William (his only bequest to a grandchild and by-passing older grandsons Joseph and George); to his daughter, Elizabeth, his share and interest in the Lewes Library Society 'for her sole and separate use and benefit'. Her previous membership, taken out on October 6, 1810, had seemingly lapsed. William's wines, liquors, consumables and housekeeping stores were left to his wife. The rest of his estate was to be divided equally between his wife, daughter, and son.

Let us now turn to his son Samuel.

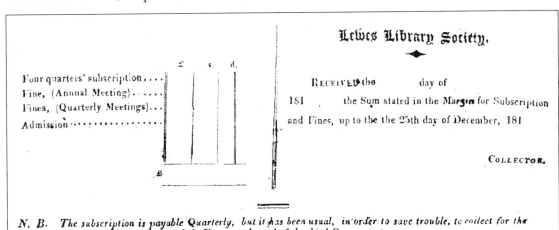

Lewes Library Society.

	£	s.	d.
Four quarters' subscription....			
Fine, (Annual Meeting)......			
Fines, (Quarterly Meetings)...			
Admission			
£			

RECEIVED the   day of
181 .   the Sum stated in the Margin for Subscription
and Fines, up to the the 25th day of December, 181

COLLECTOR.

N. B.   The subscription is payable Quarterly, but it has been usual, in order to save trouble, to collect for the whole Year, at the end of the third Quarter.

SIX

SAMUEL SMART 1799-1865
SARAH DENNETT 1804-1827
ABIGAIL EDWARDS 1804-1869

At the age of twenty-five, Samuel Hyde Smart married Sarah Jane Dennett of Southover, daughter of an old family friend. The marriage took place on September 14, 1824, at St Michael's church. As a minor Sarah needed the consent of her mother, also Sarah, the second wife to John Dennett, now a widow. John Dennett had been William's neighbour when they lived in Market Street. Originally he worked as a coal and mill stone merchant but in 1792 he became a licensed victualler at the White Horse in Station Street (then St Mary's Lane) where the Royal Oak now stands. He is mentioned in the *Lewes Town Book* as being a member of a committee set up to provide a new market place on a piece of land in the castle yard belonging to Lord Hampden. On his death John Dennett left a reasonable estate with much of it bequeathed to his daughter.

A daughter, Sarah Jane, was born to Sarah and Samuel in November 1824. But when the child was just two-and-a-half years old her mother died, and she was cared for by her grandmother, Frances Smart, and her aunt, Elizabeth Shelley, while her father toiled at the mill.

Samuel had, meanwhile, been elected

to the jury and took up his position in 1826. In the same year, after the death of George Stanford, he managed to buy the moiety (half) of his lands sold to him by the executors of Stanford's will. Following in his father's footsteps, Samuel was also elected Headborough in 1828.

On May 2, 1829, Samuel's daughter, Sarah Jane, died, aged four years, five months, and was buried next to her mother in St Michael's churchyard. To take his mind off his tremendous loss, Samuel put all his energies and emotions into his work.

Samuel, always mindful of his role in local affairs and the family business, later found time to pursue the affairs of the heart. He met a young woman, Abigail Edwards, daughter of James and Mary Edwards of Ringmer, and they were married on January 1, 1835. The couple remained childless.

Millers in the town were asked to tender for the provision of flour for the Lewes Union workhouses. The flour had to be of good quality and sold at a reasonable cost. *The Minute Book of the Lewes Guardians* records that Samuel Smart was the miller chosen. Bread was the staple diet of the workhouse and much flour would have been used.

On March 31, 1838, the *Sussex Agricultural Express* reported on a theft from Samuel Smart's home:

During the hours of divine service at St. Michael's on Sunday last some thieves effected an entrance into the dwelling house of Mr. Smart, miller and carried off a gallon of gin and an equal quantity of home made wine. It is thought that the vagabonds were disturbed in their pilfering avocation as the neighbours distinctly heard a whistle (a signal of warning among thieves) just as the congregation were leaving church.

Samuel was soon in the news again, this time in his capacity as a Town Commissioner. In April 1838 a case had been taken against Robert Neal, freeholder of the Mill House, because of his failure to comply with an Act of Parliament. This Act demanded that any person erecting new buildings, in this case four new houses in St Michael's parish, near the church, was bound to pave the land in front of the properties.

The Commissioners told magistrates that they were compelled to lay the pavements themselves at a cost of £2.18s. Neal refused to pay the whole amount, offering only £1 4s 6d. He felt he had been treated unfairly, believing that the Commissioners had paid for other people's areas to be paved. The magistrate ordered that Neal should pay the full amount with costs.

Samuel was also a Collector of the Church Rate, and in a similar instance he had demanded the money due from Henry Carter and James Palmer. Carter owed 1s 9d and 2s 1d, and Palmer two rates of 2s 10d. Palmer said that other people in the Row (Prospect Row?) had not paid and he did not see why he had to. Both men were ordered to pay the money owing within a month.

The 1841 census lists Samuel Smart, his wife Abigail and a servant, Jane Edwards, living at 75 High Street. He was overseeing the work of the mill, helped by his nephew, Joseph. George Bailey, and his family were living at 74 High Street and running the bakery.

In October, 1845, Samuel was elected Junior Constable serving with Nathan Hammond. Their remit included preparing an inventory of the borough's property, which included:

Four keys of the lock up Cell at the Engine House, One Key of the Market (in the possession of Smart) One of the stocks Two keys of the Town Chest Two of the Market Tower Five pair of Handcuffs Key of the Clock and Sundry keys.

Samuel donated money for the repair of the almshouses in Keere Street in 1846. These provided charity homes for impoverished women aged fifty years and over. In the same year he was elected to serve on the Jury.

October 1848 saw Samuel chosen as High Constable with Edwin Neal as Junior Constable. Samuel's mother, Frances, lived just long enough to see her son following in the footsteps of his father.

On June 30, 1849, Samuel, who had been elected Beadle and Surveyor – a grand title for a position that required him to look after the sanitary health of the town – was reprimanded by the Town Commissioners. It had been noted that the drains in Sun Street and St John's Street were blocked with 'obstacles'. But he failed to carry out his duties with enough vigour, resulting in other members doing his work themselves. At a Commissioners' meeting in October he was asked to resign. After lengthy discussion it was finally agreed that the job would be advertised at £30 a year and that Samuel be allowed to stay on as Assistant Surveyor, on a salary of £10 a year, for a further twelve months. The matter did not rest. A resident in All Saints' parish wrote to the *Sussex Agricultural Express* complaining about Smart's attitude to his post. He reminded readers that in 1832, when the county was infected with cholera, not one person had died in Lewes, due to the careful attention to sanitation and hygiene of the then Commissioners. He continued:

If we had a responsible and efficient surveyor in office he would not have left the Commissioners in ignorance of pig pounds vehicles carrying noxious waste from slaughter houses. Smart could have evoked an Act of Parliament, that pigs should not be kept in the walls of the city or town!

The Commissioners were incensed that Smart had let them down and there were those who believed that he was being absolved of his negligence only 'in consequence of his past rather than his present services'. One moment Smart was meeting and organising with the gentry, the next he was being pilloried for his negligence of a far less salubrious task.

The 1851 census records Samuel and Abigail still at 75 High Street, with a new servant girl, Elizabeth Turner, aged sixteen, who came from Hamsey. Business continued to grow although there was healthy competition from other millers in the town. Samuel now employed three men and a baker's boy,

William Shoesmith, to help in the running of his prosperous business.

In his year of office as High Constable, 1848, Samuel had overseen the bringing of the Royal Agricultural Show to the town. An initial contact was made between the secretary to the Royal Agricultural Society and Smart and Neal in March 1849, to consider the proposition. Guildford and Maidstone were also proposed, but Lewes won the honour of holding the event. On June 2 a public meeting was held with the Constables and Headboroughs to discuss proposals in greater detail. At the conclusion a large party of local dignitaries retired to the Public Rooms in West Street where they sat down to a cold collation. Then the party adjourned to tread the boundaries of the ancient borough and to walk off very full stomachs.

Many a long night was passed as meetings were held to thrash out all the organisational problems, including where the event should be held, provision of transport for people, animals and goods etc. Access to the site by rail was examined, maintenance of law and order discussed as well as many other problems which needed to be addressed in organising such a prestigious event. Subscriptions were raised throughout the town and surrounding areas. Samuel Smart set the tone for the local trades-people by donating the sum of £25. A total of £1,000 was raised in the town and a similar amount from the nobility and gentry of the county. The South Coast Railway Company gave £500.

On April 28, 1852, local dignitaries and the chief officers met a deputation from the Royal Agricultural Society to view the chosen site, which included the Priory grounds, the Ham and Hither Rise in Southover, and the Wallands. County Hall, the Star Inn and the Corn Exchange were thought suitable as venues for lectures, dinners and committee meetings.

The show opened on the July 12, 1852, and ran for four days. Complementing the show was a town-organised horticultural exhibition on the Castle Bowling Green and in Castle Precincts on July 14-16. To be sure of having the finest exhibits, in fruit, flowers and vegetables, all classes had been advertised in trade papers, local papers and papers circulating in Brighton. Samuel Smart, astute enough to see the possibility of increased trade in the town, was one of the signatories who underwrote the event to the tune of £5.

After the excitement and involvement in the two major events in the town, Samuel had to turn his attention to his own work. Smart's Mill was in trouble again, with the wind flow impeded by the building of the new gaol on adjacent land. In 1853, it was necessary to heighten the round house by 20ft to lift the smock and sweeps to catch the winds. At the same time the smock was painted white. The total cost of the work was £150. It was carried out by Samuel Medhurst, son of William Medhurst, who had the original job of removing the smock from the Town Mill

site for the very same reason.

It would appear that security was a little lax at the mill as *The Sussex Weekly Advertiser* of January 25, 1953, reported that it had been broken into and three bushels of flour stolen.

Robert Neal, the freeholder of Mill

Samuel Smart

House and other nearby properties, died in 1855. His properties, including:

A convenient Dwelling House and Outbuildings with two pieces of garden ground, situate near lot 1 in the Parish of

St. Michael's known as the Mill House, now in occupation of Mrs. Shelley, at the yearly rent of £3. 3s' and 'a Range of Seven Cottages . . . known as Prospect Row, in the occupation of Messrs Pearce, Adams and others . . .

were put up for auction at the White Hart Hotel on March 27, 1855. Remembering the terms of his father's will, Samuel Smart bid on behalf of his widowed sister, Elizabeth, and secured the freehold of the Mill House for £85.

On October 12, 1855, Samuel Smart was appointed to the Burial Board of St Michael's to replace William Langridge who had resigned. Samuel was one of a committee who held the responsibility for managing the St Michael's area of Lewes Cemetery.

Returning to the home and more domestic affairs, we find that Samuel had accounts with Davey's Plumbers and Painters, on the High Street. In 1855 he had his carriage varnished and plumbing works done at Reads Cottage. Samuel is recorded in the Lewes Water Works ledger as having one of the largest share holdings in the company, amounting to the handsome sum of £284 10s.

In 1859 the Constables of the Borough, Richard Lambe and Charles Parsons, drew up an agreement with Samuel Smart in which he granted them permission to install a window and a waste pipe in a lavatory, in 76 High Street, the house owned by the Steere Exhibition charity. As the property overlooked his home, Smart was to receive the princely sum of a penny a year for allowing this. At any such time that Smart wanted to change the agreement, the Constables were to be given a week's notice and the window and waste pipe would be removed immediately.

When the 1861 census was taken Samuel Smart, aged sixty-one, was classified as a Master Miller living in the family property on the High Street with his wife, Abigail, aged fifty-seven. They were entertaining Francis Manser, aged seventy, a fellow master miller who had come to Lewes from his home in Dalston, Middlesex. Anne Paine, aged twenty-eight, accompanied him on his visit. A servant girl, Jane Goddard, only thirteen-years-old, was working for the

The Steere bursary

The Steere Exhibition was a charitable bursary, set up in the Reverend George Steere's will, whereby money was allocated to help a male student to study at Oxford or Cambridge for four years. The money was raised from rentals of properties at 76 High Street and from two houses in St Martin's Lane, all abutting on to the Smart/Shelley houses. Samuel Smart was one of four of 'the most able inhabitants' who were signatories on an 1855 document awarding a Steere Exhibition to William Ridge Greenhill, son of Henry Greenhill who had died, and whose mother was unable to send her son to university without this financial help.

Smarts as a maid of all work. There is a strong possibility that Jane was placed in the household straight from the workhouse. Life in her new home may not have differed too much from her life in her previous abode.

Mrs Beeton in *The Book of Household Management*, wrote: 'The housemaid who studies her own ease will certainly be at her work by six o'clock in the summer, and, probably, half past six or seven in the winter months, having spent a reasonable time in her own chamber in dressing. Earlier than this would probably, be an unnecessary waste of coals and candles in winter.'

Life was surely hard for poor Jane. After rising early it would be her responsibility to get the fires lit and hot water taken up to her master and mistress and their guests. She would then prepare breakfast and when the meal was finished she would wash the dishes. All day long there would be a strict routine of household chores to work through that would be exhausting and perhaps make her yearn for the days when she had a little more time for herself.

Samuel's sister, Elizabeth, died in the cold winter of February 1864, leaving a daughter, Sarah Jane, aged twenty. Samuel, now aged sixty-six and in failing health, retired from the Burial Board on May 26, 1865 and his nephew, Joseph Shelley, was elected in his place. On August 11 of the same year, Samuel Smart, still fighting for his rights, went to court and, represented by his nephew, Joseph, took out a summons against Richard Butcher, tenant of his property in St Martin's Lane, who had been given three month's notice to quit. The defendant pleaded that he was entitled to six months' notice. As there was no written evidence to support Samuel Smart's claim, the case was found against him and the tenant was allowed to stay.

Samuel Smart died on October 29, 1865, from 'softening of the brain and paralysis'. A fine tribute to him was carried in the *Sussex Express*:

DEATH of Mr. S. HIDE SMART – This old and respected inhabitant of St. Michael's died on Wednesday last after a long illness, which he bore with great patience and resignation. Mr. S Smart was about twenty years ago one of the High Constables of the Borough, and was, perhaps, more instrumental in bringing the Royal Agricultural Society to Lewes than any other gentleman in the town. The large amount required from the town almost staggered our leading men, but, on hearing that Mr. Smart declared he would himself subscribe £50 to the fund, they felt that if that was to be the spirit to be evinced by the trade generally, the venture might fairly be made. This striking proof of public spirit did not pass unnoticed at the time. We may add that in his business relations with the poor, Mr Smart ever proved himself a kind friend, and we may add though in a business in which the resort to the County Court is very common, he never in his life even took a summons against a debtor. This was by no means the result of adhering to the ready money system. On the contrary, he gave unbounded credit to the poor, and had to submit to the usual, or more than usual losses in these cases. He never allowed these, however, to interfere with his usual practice, and his faith often met with an unexpected reward. On one occasion the story runs that a Wesleyan minister, many years ago, left Lewes about £20 in his debt. He never pressed for the amount, and about ten years after the debt was incurred he was astonished one fine morning with a cheque, which was duly honoured, for the full amount.

After her husband's funeral and affairs had been put in order, Abigail returned to Ringmer where she had lived before her marriage. She died on December 17, 1869, four years after her husband's death. Her body was returned to Lewes and interred in the Smart family tomb in St Michael's. It sits in the centre of the churchyard, nestling snugly under a sycamore tree and chronicles the deaths of the Smart and Shelley families:

In loving memory of SARAH JANE, the wife of Samuel Hyde Smart who died on May 14th 1827 aged 24 years also to the memory of WILLIAM SMART late of this parish who died 14th July 1837 aged 66 years, also of SARAH daughter of SAMUEL HYDE SMART and SARAH JANE SMART who died April 2nd 1829 aged 4 years 5 months. In memory of FRANCES relict of WILLIAM SMART late of this parish who died 4th January 1849 aged 87 years. In memory of FRANCES daughter of JOSEPH and ELIZABETH SHELLEY who died September 24th 1827 aged 6 years.

Sadly, the inscriptions on the tomb have worn away but it is still possible to read Abigail's name on the end panel.

The death of Abigail brought the Smart family line to an end. Samuel was a successful and a wealthy man leaving an estate valued at £4,000. There was no issue from either of his marriages to benefit from his financial expertise.

Let us now take a sideways look into the lives of Joseph and his wife, Elizabeth, who benefited from some of Samuel's business acumen.

SEVEN

JOSEPH SHELLEY 1788-1845
ELIZABETH SMART 1795-1864

You can see Lewes lying like a box of toys under a green amphitheatre of chalk hills. On the whole it is set down better than any town I have seen in England.
William Morris

Joseph was born to John and Elizabeth Shelley in 1788 at 166 High Street, Lewes. His grandfather, John Shelley, and his father worked together in the prosperous family business as carriers. *Bailey's British Directory* of 1784 lists it as Shelley and Son Carriers. An early business card informs customers that the vehicles were 'Original Stage Waggons', that no responsibility was accepted for the safe delivery of goods and insurance was recommended. In 1805, the Shelley family had built the business up successfully and held the monopoly on the route from London to Lewes.

Travel was slow due to the poor conditions of the roads and a journey from London to Brighton, a distance of fifty miles, could take up to five hours.

The carrier would of necessity work a very long day, loading up with goods at first light; harnessing the horses to the waggon and setting off on what could be a perilous journey through all kinds of weathers. On arrival, the goods would be unloaded and delivered to those waiting and then the whole process would be repeated for the homeward journey. The local papers often tell of horses getting out of control, waggons

LEWES & LONDON
Original Stage Waggons,

BY SHELLEY,

Load at the GEORGE INN, Borough, every WEDNESDAY, *and at the WHITE HART, INN, Borough every* SATURDAY.

Forward Goods to the undermentioned Places:

LEWES,	BLATCHINGTON,	FIRLE,	STANMER,
NEWHAVEN,	ALFRISTON,	GLYNDE,	OFFHAM,
SEAFORD,	WILMINGTON,	RINGMER,	CHAILEY,

AND ALL PLACES ADJACENT.

The above Waggons set out from LEWES, every MONDAY and, THURSDAY Morning.

The Proprietor will not be accountable for any Money, Plate, Watches, Writings, Jewels, Glass, or China, however small the value may be, unless an Insurance be paid above the common rate of Carriage. Nor more than Five Pounds will be paid for any one Package of other Goods, not specified above, except entered & paid for accordingly. Will not be accountable for any accident that may happen to Carriages drawn at the end of the Waggons; nor any live Animal, though lost, hurt, or killed.

Shelley's trade card, printed by Baxter.

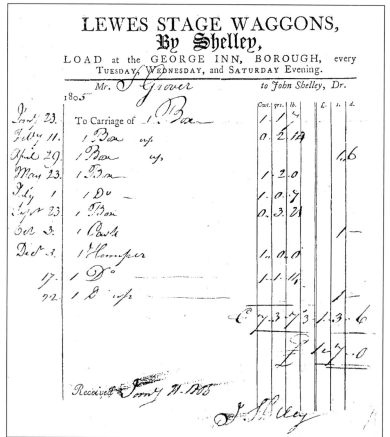

LEWES STAGE WAGGONS,
By Shelley,

LOAD at the GEORGE INN, BOROUGH, every
TUESDAY, WEDNESDAY, and SATURDAY Evening.

Mr. Grover   to John Shelley, Dr.

A Shelley invoice.

being overturned and drivers and passengers being seriously hurt. This, coupled with the danger of highwaymen lurking on isolated roads, made it a dangerous occupation and not for the faint-hearted.

In 1812, John Shelley and his family, were recorded as still living at 166 High Street. Around this date the houses at 165, 166, and 167 High Street were demolished and replaced by Castle Place, which was to become the home of Dr Gideon Mantell and his wife.

Towards the end of 1812, Joseph's father, John Shelley started work on Brack Mound House, which was to have the convenience of its own waggon shed. It was built on a piece of land that belonged to John's father and was subject to the annual manorial rent of two shillings, payable on the feast of St Michael the Archangel. In the footnotes to "A Lewes Diary 1916-1944" there is reference to the property built in 1813 as a watch tower by the London-Lewes carrier, John Shelley. It stands against the second motte of Lewes Castle. Horsfield also refers to Shelley's property "The south wall of Mr Shelley's warehouse on the Castle bank is a portion of the old fortification that has been newly faced".

Following his marriage to Elizabeth Smart, in 1819, Joseph Shelley continued to run the family business: *Pigot's Directory* of 1828/29, advertises:

Joseph Shelley, carrier, leaving from his office on the High Street, every Tuesday, Thursday and Saturday.

As a religious dissenter, Joseph could not be actively involved in local government, as were his father-in-law and brother-in-law; this activity, and the right to attend university, was denied to all dissenters, who often put their energies into good works.

On the domestic front, 1821 saw the birth of the Shelley's first child, a girl called Frances, named after her maternal grandmother.

In St Martin's Lane Elizabeth gave

birth to a son, Joseph, on March 19, 1823, followed by George, the following year, and a daughter, Elizabeth, on December 13, 1825. The names Elizabeth, Joseph, William, Frances and Francis, were used frequently in the Shelley family.

On June 4, 1827, Elizabeth bore twins, William and Ellen. Just three months later, the couple's first born, Frances, died, aged six years – a painful reminder of William and Frances Smart's own first born, Frances, who had died in infancy.

In 1829 Joseph's father sold the carrier business to John Jarratt, a rival company. This left Joseph without any paid work to maintain his ever-increasing family. In 1831, he found a position as a stationer, possibly working for his brother, Thomas, who was a herald painter. Now with six growing children to feed and clothe, Joseph found it increasingly difficult to manage financially.

The first entry in the Westgate Minute Book, written by the minister, Charles Porteous Valentine, records that the Reverend W Johnstone had bequeathed £20 to the Westgate Chapel congregation to be used to purchase goods for those in dire need. Joseph Shelley received a 'half chaldron of Cloke' (coke) to warm his home in an attempt to keep the dreaded tuberculosis at bay. The fuel was valued at £1.10s.

Joseph Shelley was a worshipper with the Dissenting Presbyterians at the Meeting House in Eastport Lane, Lewes. Many of the congregation moved to the Westgate Chapel in the years 1825-26 and accepted a Unitarian system of belief that tended to attract people of a liberal and radical tradition.

Possibly the most famous member of the chapel was Thomas Paine, author of *Rights of Man*. Thomas Horsfield, the writer, historian and one-time pastor of Westgate, was among other intellectuals of the middle and lower artisan class who chose to worship at Westgate Chapel. Considerable numbers of the faithful were from trade, some of whom went on to hold public office. Working and caring for others was considered an integral part of the faith. The ethos behind Unitarianism was that all beliefs were of equal merit and should be treated with unreserved respect. Each person was encouraged to seek out what he or she considered was right and true and was not required to adhere to any preordained creed laid down by a church hierarchy. Unitarians repudiated the divinity of Christ and original sin and, unlike in many other Christian faiths, they held progressive views on the role of women in society.

As yet another baby arrived, Joseph found it increasingly difficult to support, feed and clothe his nine children. His name appears in 'An Account of the Money Collected and Distributed on Behalf of the Poor Connected with the Protestant Dissenting Congregation of Lewes', dated 1835:

August: 5s 0d given to Joseph Shelley due to Illness.

Elizabeth had given birth to Fanny Hide on August 14 that year, and it may have been her baby who needed help. With all their high ideals about helping the poor, Joseph and Elizabeth's close family appeared to do nothing to help. One is left wondering what on earth was going on in this family. Were they not ashamed to allow poverty to plague them, without offering them a helping hand. It seems that Elizabeth did not have a live-in servant or nursery maid, there was certainly no one listed on the 1841 census. She may have had to depend on her mother or her eldest daughter, Elizabeth, who was only ten years old, for help in running the household and for tending to the younger children. The *Poll Book* for 1837 gives Joseph's address as Western Terrace, indicating that a move from St Martin's Lane to the Round House had been made. Evidently, a conversion from the mill round house had been made but it is difficult, almost impossible, to think how a family of this size could live in such a cramped space.

The 1837 Poll Book reveals that Joseph had a new occupation as a writer. But what sort of writer? The Oxford English Dictionary came up with a viable suggestion, a sign writer. It is just feasible that Joseph and his brother, Thomas, were working together on gilding and sign-writing on trade coaches and coaches belonging to the gentry.

John Shelley, Joseph's father, died at his home on August 31, 1838, aged seventy-nine. The cause of death was given as old age. He was buried in the Eastport Lane Meeting House, next to his wife, Elizabeth, who had died on May 27, 1833. Their memorial stone lists the deaths of their daughters, Maria, who had died in 1803, aged three, Mary Ann, 1820, in her sixteenth year and Elizabeth, wife of William Figg, cartographer, who died on September 12, 1840, without bearing any children.

John Shelley's eldest son, Henry, had the responsibility of distributing his father's assets in accordance with his will. The sum of £600 was left to Henry and to John, the younger. His daughters, Harriet and Elizabeth, and son, Robert, were to be given £300 each; sons Joseph and Thomas, and daughter, Sarah, received £200. The residue of his estate was to be shared between Henry and

John's three daughters.

John Shelley's property was put up for auction, at the Star Inn, Lewes, on November 10, 1838, in accordance with the terms of his will. The auctioneers were Verrall & Son. The advertisement, for the property at Brack Mound, read:

Two good dwelling Houses with a Garden: an extensive range of stabling which is convertible for Buildings of any description. A MOST comfortable roomy and substantially-built DWELLING HOUSE, very pleasantly situate near the bowling green, within the Precincts of the Lewes Castle, being extra parochial and consequently nearly free from Local and Parochial Taxes, with a walk in garden, late in the occupation of the said Mr. John Shelley; also a small neat Dwelling House adjoining, in the occupation of Mr. George Leney; and a roomy and an extensive range of stabling, with lofts over, in the occupation of Mr. Jarratt. The above property has great capability of being converted into dwelling houses, having an extensive frontage, the situation being particularly pleasant, with the advantage of being extra parochial and also commanding Votes for the Borough of Lewes.

Joseph was a man who had experienced poverty at first hand, knew the misery that it caused and was aware that an empty belly could lead to crime. He organised the collection of money to provide a soup kitchen for the hungry of St Michael's parish. Those in need were given a daily ticket that entitled them to a pint of hot, nourishing soup. Brother-in-law, John Figg, provided the basic ingredients from his grocer's shop at 77 High Street. Samuel, keen to be seen to be helping, donated 2s 6d to the collection. George Bailey, baker at 74 High Street, probably provided stale

A nineteenth century soup kitchen similar to that organised by the Shelleys.

bread to accompany the soup.

In the 1841 census the names of people were recorded for the first time and their places of birth also listed. Where they were literate enough, the householders filled in their own census forms for the first time. The census record informs that the Shelley family had returned to the family property in St Martin's Lane, vacated on the death of William Smart.

St Michael's Pa.... Soup Ticket

Deliver to

Pint of Soup

By order of the Committee

A daily ticket for the soup kitchen

Frances, William's widow, had moved in with Elizabeth and Joseph Shelley and their eight children.

Elizabeth, who was then fifteen, worked as a dressmaker's apprentice; Joseph, eighteen, was learning the art of milling in the family business. Ellen, fourteen, Francis, twelve, Harry, ten, Richard, nine, Fanny six and Edward, four, were all listed as scholars.

When she was forty-nine, Elizabeth discovered that she was pregnant yet again. One can only imagine how devastated she felt. Her last child, Edward, had been born seven years before. But there was nothing that could be done and Sarah Jane, named after Sarah and Samuel's daughter, was born in 1844.

Less than a year later, on September 3, 1845, Joseph died, aged fifty-seven. His death certificate recorded his death in the sub-district of Chailey and gives the cause of death as 'epilepsy (not certified)'. Was it his 'epileptic behaviour' that caused the suspected tensions with his father and brother-in-law, who may have seen it as madness,

55

evil and dangerous? Is there anything significant in the fact that Sarah Marten was the informant of his death and not his wife Elizabeth? It should be mentioned that she was a worshipper at the Meeting House in Eastport Lane and was no doubt a friend of the family. Joseph was buried in the yard of the Meeting House, where his parents were interred. No memorial stone was placed to commemorate his life.

Ellen, daughter of Joseph and Elizabeth, like her sister, Elizabeth, trained as a dressmaker. Ellen was living away from home, in Old Market Lane, Lewes, when she contracted tuberculosis and died on May 28, 1848, aged twenty-one. Her death certificate records the cause of death as 'Phshisis Pulmonalis'. At this time tuberculosis was a killer. It affected a large percentage of the population, particularly in the overcrowded, densely populated urban areas. Some early research suggested that the disease was hereditary. It certainly was to take its relentless toll on the Shelley family.

Their son, William, was the first member of his family to move to Brighton, where he married Mary Ann Page on August 27, 1849.

Elizabeth Shelley was given the responsibility of caring for her aged mother, Frances, following the death of William, her father, in 1837. This could not have been an easy job for her with such a large family to look after. Frances lived to the venerable age of eighty-seven, dying in January 1849. She was put to rest in the family tomb.

Fanny Hide, aged sixteen, died on the January 11, 1851, at the Mill House. Her mother, Elizabeth, held her daughter in her arms as she took her last pitiful gasps and died from tuberculosis. The 1851 census shows that, Elizabeth was now living with four of her children – Elizabeth, twenty-five; Harry, an apprentice shoemaker (who later moved to Jersey Street in Brighton, where he died in 1861; (his body was returned to Lewes and buried in the town cemetery).

Elizabeth Shelley wife of Joseph 1858

Edward, who was training as a miller with his Uncle Samuel, also died in the Mill House from tuberculosis, aged only twenty-one, on July 11, 1858. Edward was buried close to his brother and their mother, Elizabeth, when she died in 1864.

On this sad note let us turn to new beginnings and find out about Elizabeth and Joseph's sons and daughters, ordinary people, who went on to make some significant contributions to their family, to Lewes and, in some ways, their country.

EIGHT

JOSEPH SHELLEY AND EMMA BLUNDEN
GEORGE SHELLEY AND MARY TESTER
FRANCIS SHELLEY AND HARRIET WEST

Joseph, George and Francis, sons of Joseph and Elizabeth Shelley, have been singled out so that their lives may be explored in more detail because of the contributions they made to local politics, the church and the welfare of the town of Lewes. Passing references will be made to their extended families who must not be ignored because they were all part of the family tapestry.

The brothers' early lives were not easy because of the financial problems that beset their parents as the family grew in size. Joseph was the second child, born in March 1823, following his sister Frances, born in October 1821 and who died in 1827. George was born fourteen months later, in 1824, and Francis in 1828. There were six young children dependent on their parents in the period up until 1829 when Joseph sold his father's carrier business. Where the family was living at that time is not clearly documented, but it is known that by 1837 they were living in the unextended Mill House, with ten children, including two infants. With the death of William Smart in 1837 there was some financial relief. William had left his daughter well provided for but Joseph had been left the paltry amount of five shillings a week, at the discretion of the trustees, and no other bequests of property or goods. However, William had safeguarded the future of his grand-children, which would be a relief to their parents.

Life would have continued to improve as the children began work and were able to supplement the family income. The 1841 census shows that young Joseph had been apprenticed as a miller, his eldest sister, Elizabeth, was an apprentice dressmaker, George and Francis were still at school.

Joseph senior died in 1845 leaving his wife to bring up five children still living at home.

With their financial and educational futures secured by their grandfather, the three young men, all living away from home, were now able to turn their thoughts to marriage. All three Shelley sons found their brides in Brighton. There was a flurry of weddings, George married Mary, daughter of Henry Tester, grocer on May 14, 1849, in the Church of St Nicholas, Brighton; Joseph married Emma Louise Blunden in 1849 and Francis married Harriet West in 1850.

George and Mary moved into 74 High Street, with their baby, William, born on May 1, 1850. He was looked after by Fanny Holland aged just twelve, who was also a maid of all work. Downstairs, George Bailey continued to run the bakery business until about 1855. George Shelley specialised in confectionery.

Joseph and Emma occupied one of the adjoining cottages in St Martins Lane. Joseph worked at his Uncle Samuel's mill. Emma gave birth to their first baby, on February 2, 1850 – a daughter Ellen, named in memory of Joseph's sister who had recently died. Mary Brayant from Ringmer, aged thirteen, was employed as a nurse girl to help take care of the baby.

Francis did not join the family business, preferring to work in the printing trade. He was an apprentice compositor under George Bacon, owner of the *Sussex Advertiser,* and at the end of his apprenticeship he joined the *Sussex Express* as a reader.

The photographer Edward Reeves set up his new studios at 159 High Street in 1858 and Joseph Shelley was one of his earliest customers (number 172, in the Reeves account book). The photographs taken at this date were known as *carte de visite* after the Parisian photographer, Andre Disderi, started the fashion for using the *cartes* as calling cards. They were introduced to England in 1858. Photographs were usually taken to mark a right of passage and times of importance for the family. Both the sitter's costume and the photographers' props are useful in dating photographs, although fashions were slower to change in the country towns.

The photograph of Joseph is interesting on different levels. His grubby clothing and floury shoes suggest that he has come directly from the mill, and his dishevelled hair, that he had forgotten his comb. The photograph, taken against the backcloth of the Ouse and the castle,

is posed to suggest a man of the town. If you look carefully to the rear of his legs, you will see that he is held in position by a photographic stand and his right hand

Joseph Shelley in milling clothes, 1858.

rests against a support on top of the pillar, both necessary to aid the subject through a long exposure.

Returning to the three brothers, Joseph, George and Francis – they, like their grandfather, William Smart, and to a lesser extent, their father, Joseph, were all to take an active role in local politics and in the religious and social welfare of the town. All three men had allegiance to St Michael's but gradually embraced the

Dissenters' beliefs, and worshipped at the Westgate Unitarian Chapel in Lewes.

Elizabeth Shelley, the eldest daughter of Joseph and Elizabeth, left Lewes to live in Hastings following her marriage to William Branch at the Westgate Chapel on September 11, 1853. She gave birth to their first child, yet another William, in 1854. The couple returned to Lewes for the baptism of their baby at Westgate Chapel, and in 1887 they took up residence in Lewes. William Shelley Branch opened a photographic and stationary shop at 16-16a High Street, but it seemed that the family continued to give their patronage to Edward Reeves.

The 1850s were a prolific time for the Shelley families. Thirteen babies were born to the wives of Joseph, George and Francis, including a set of twins, Louisa and Fanny, born to Joseph and Emma in 1857. Louisa died the following year just after her first birthday. The Westgate Baptism register lists all the babies as they were received into the church.

In 1852 and 1853 Burial Acts had been passed, before which most people were buried in their local churchyards, but with a fifty per cent increase in population, churchyards became overcrowded and were regarded as health hazards. Bodies of the poor were often stolen from the shallow graves, under the cover of darkness and sold for medical dissection. The Burial Acts enabled local authorities to open their own designated cemeteries and banned burials in churchyards and vaults in cities. The St Michael's Vestry notes record the setting up of the Burial Board with elected members who had to be ratepayers. At a meeting in the Brewer's Arms on July 21, 1853, both George and Joseph Shelley were among the parishioners who were given the task of finding additional burial grounds in Lewes. It was decided that the simplest way to deal with the problem was to approach the other seven parishes in the town and work together. There was a fair degree of urgency, as the government demanded that all burial grounds connected to churches be closed by July 1, 1853.

For reasons of their own the other parishes declined to join St Michael's in obtaining a piece of land, and so St Michael's bought two and a half acres solely for the use of its own parishioners, from John Verrall. The price was £600. Once the burial site was arranged, the Select Vestry Committee drew up a table of fees and payments for the interment of bodies.

Other parishes obtained burial ground later, and Lewes Cemetery consists of the St Michael's site, opened in 1854, and a second site for the combined parishes of All Saints and St Thomas, opened in 1873.

Joseph Shelley made his debut in public life in 1856 and began what was to be a long and dedicated service to the people of Lewes. In that year he was elected Headborough, served on the Jury and was elected to the St Michael's Burial Board. Joseph and Emma had a second child, Emma, born in 1855, and a third, Francis, in 1856.

1858 proved to be a difficult year for Joseph and Emma Shelley as two-year-old Francis died on March 30 from hydrocephalus, and Louisa, one of the twins, died, aged one, from tuberculosis. The two babies have their own little plot in the St Michael's area of the cemetery.

In April of that year, Joseph was appointed a churchwarden to

St Michael's. His duties included the upkeep of the church fabric, helping to keep the parish registers up-to-date and in good order, arranging for the burial of itinerants and the baptism of foundlings, allocating the pews for worship, even the extermination of vermin in the church.

At about the same time a proposal by the Constables was set in motion to build swimming baths in the Town Brook area of Lewes. Residents were keen to have a safe and clean place to bathe. Subscriptions were quickly raised with the two MPs, JG Blencowe and the Hon H Brand, making generous donations of £25 each. A grand total of £442 5s 6d was raised by the townspeople.

For reasons unknown the Smart and Shelley families, always generous in public subscription, gave nothing to the fund, but later took out season tickets.

Wealthy members of the community able to make a donation of £5 were given life membership. The swimming pool at The Pells was open to all in 1860. But the bathers were strictly segregated, men having prime use of the facilities every day, including a three-hour session on Sundays. Women were restricted to three sessions a week

Harriet Shelley

Francis Shelley

that had to be taken in the mornings. Children under twelve were not allowed to use the pool for longer than half an hour, but were admitted at the reduced rate of 3d and could have a season ticket for the open shed for 2s 6d.

Joseph Shelley bought a season ticket shortly after the pool opened. George Shelley, his brother, his son, William Harry and nephew, William, bought season tickets in 1865.

The Pells Pool, as it is now known, is said to be the oldest open-air swimming pool in the country and remains a great asset to the town.

In 1861 Joseph Shelley lived in the High Street with his wife, Emma. He was thirty-eight, a baker listed as employing one man and one boy. He and Emma were by now the parents of seven children – Ellen, eleven; Joseph, nine; William, eight; Emma, six; Francis, five, Fanny, three and baby, Frank, a year old. Nursery nurse Anne Knight, who was fifteen, was employed to help to look after the youngest children.

In the Mill House was Joseph's mother, Elizabeth, aged sixty-six and still actively involved in the families' lives as a grandmother and as a 'proprietress of houses'. Her youngest daughter, Sarah, was still living at home and not working. A girl, Mary Green aged fifteen, was employed as a general housemaid.

Francis and Harriet had moved out of the family homes on the High Street and in St Martin's Lane and were living in North Street. Francis was employed as a publisher's advertising clerk.

On January 28, 1864, Elizabeth died and was buried, not with her husband in the Meeting House yard, but in the St Michael's area of the cemetery. Nine months after her death, Samuel sold the Mill House, on October 24, 1864, to his nephew, Francis Shelley, for £150. On the same day as the sale, Elizabeth, just eight-months-old, the youngest daughter of Joseph and Emma, died at home from hydrocephalus. She was placed in the grave with her grandmother.

The photograph of Emma Shelley is taken with baby

Emma Shelley with her baby daughter Elizabeth, who shared a grave with her grandmother.

Elizabeth in late 1863. Mrs Shelley is wearing a black crinoline dress, bonnet and a cameo brooch, possibly mourning dress as baby Walter, her son, had died in 1863 from a bout of influenza. The baby is wearing copious white petticoats and an embroidered overdress. She has little bracelet on her left arm. Her swollen head is characteristic of the hydrocephalus that killed her shortly after the photograph was taken.

Joseph and Elizabeth's youngest daughter, Sarah, born just before the death of her father, was married to Herbert Whiteman, eldest son of Randall Whiteman, at the Unitarian Chapel, Cranbrook, on June 15, 1866. The Reverend Richard Shelley, Sarah's brother, conducted the wedding. Richard had trained as a bookbinder in Lewes before training for the ministry at the Presbyterian College in Carmarthen, in 1853. After his ordination he went to a parish in Shepton Mallet, followed by a five year living at Newbury. He took a four-year sabbatical and during that time he officiated at the baptism of Elizabeth Frances, born to his sister-in-law, Harriet, and brother, Francis, in May 1865 at the Westgate Chapel. His last ministry was in Yarmouth where he had married and fathered two children. One, Arrowsmith Hide Shelley, eventually followed him into the church. Richard Shelley died in Newbury on April 18, 1873, aged forty.

Sarah and Herbert Whiteman left Lewes to live in London but came back to the Wesleyan Chapel for the baptism of their first child, Edith Jane, on December 5, 1869.

The 1867 *Lewes Post Office Directory* listed George Shelley as a grocer and baker in Richard Alderton's shop in Keere Street. Joseph, having succeeded his uncle, Samuel Smart, was working the mill which was now known as Shelley's Mill.

Samuel Smart's estate was worth just under £4,000, a considerable sum for a man in trade and that was before the sale of his properties and his lands were completed. Some were not offered for sale until after the death of his wife in 1869. Verrall & Son, auctioneers, put up the first lot of properties on November 16, 1866, at the Star Inn. The *East Sussex News* reported that the auction was well attended and business brisk. Seven lots were offered, four of property and three of shares in Lewes Water Company.

Lot 1 was of two freehold dwellings, namely 74 and 75 High Street, let to Joseph Shelley at a rent of £30 a year. Interest was keen and the bidding rapid until the houses were knocked down to Joseph Shelley for £505.

Sarah Shelley, daughter of Elizabeth and Joseph, 1858, aged fourteen.

Lot 2, a freehold dwelling in St Martin's Lane was let on a monthly tenancy to Mr Butcher. Joseph Shelley, who had been unsuccessful in giving the tenant notice to quit in the proceeding year, bought this house for £190.

Lot 3 was two freehold cottages bringing in a rent of £14 6s, and a stable let to Joseph Shelley. George Shelley bought this lot for £260.

Lot 4 was a freehold dwelling house in Eastport Lane said to be suitable for further extension. This was bought by C Stanford, the son of builder George Stanford, who had been involved in buying meadowland with William Smart back in the 1820s.

The last three lots were £25 shares in Lewes Water Company, all sold to a Mr Carter, the first two at £70 each, and the third at £68.

Meanwhile, two years earlier, Francis Shelley, with two new babies to feed and clothe, was forced to mortgage the Mill House with his neighbour, Alfred Hammond, a brazier and tinman, for £100 at five per cent interest. Francis may have taken out the mortgage to pay for works needed on the Mill House. The thatched roof was still in place when Andrew Nash did a pencil sketch of Lewes Castle in 1848, but at some later

*Lewes Castle from the Paddock, a pencil sketch dated 1848 by Andrew Nash.
The Round House is shown with a thatched roof and a small extension.*

date this had been replaced with a pitched, eight-faceted tiled roof. An extension was built consisting of a linking stair well and two rooms, one on the ground floor, one above. There is nothing in the deeds to indicate when these changes were made, but the Ordnance Survey map of 1873 shows the extension in place. This loan was paid off by October 27, 1870, and a reconveyance of the property was completed.

Sadness came to 74 High Street when Emma, the thirteen-year-old daughter of Joseph and Emma, died on June 18, 1868 from tuberculosis. She had suffered from the disease for about nine months and wasted away in front of her family. Her photograph, taken about 1867, shows her to be a beautiful and bonny girl, just her tell-tale dark eyes showing that she was already unwell.

More of Samuel's lands and dwellings came up for sale on Tuesday, May 31,

Emma Shelley at thirteen

1870, at the Star Inn. There were five lots.

Lot 1 was several pieces of freehold brookland, near to the Anchor Inn at Barcombe, including accommodation made up of 'a four roomed brick built cottage, a washhouse, dairy, cow lodge, piggery, slated bullock-lodge, rick yard, and garden'. The apportioned rent was £46 a year. George Heaves of Isfield bought the lot for £1,380.

Lot 2 was 'an excellent freehold brookland with cow shed and rick yard' lying between the Anchor Inn and the Lewes-Uckfield rail line. The rent was £12 a year. Frederick Smith of Sutton Hurst bought this parcel of land for £370, and with it he purchased Lot 3 for £360.

63

This was 'a piece of freehold brookland, situated in Barcombe separated from Lot 2 by the railway'.

Lot 4 was freehold brookland with 'a brick-built, slat-healed lodge', sold to by William and Francis Verrall, brewers, for £270.

Lot 5 was an acre of brookland in the Ham of Southover with a frontage to the Cockshut Stream, sold to Joseph Shelley for £220.

In line with the rest of the country Lewes was developing rapidly and becoming increasingly industrialised. By 1871 there were seven breweries, three racing stables and four iron foundries, a candle factory, soap factories, gasworks, tanneries and other industries growing up close to the Ouse. New housing was built with the well-to-do families moving away from the smoke of the town to the leafy areas of the Wallands. Housing for the workers in the new industries was built in New Road and in the Cliffe. The Bank Holiday Act of the same year laid down legislation establishing paid holidays for workers.

Francis Shelley's family was settled in the Mill House when the 1871 census was taken on April 2. He was still working as a printer's clerk but was seeking a change in his career away from the print trade. His wife Harriet cared for their living children, Harriet, aged eighteen, who was still at home, Gertrude, twelve, Edith Helen, nine, Amy Alice, six and Arthur, five months, and mourned for her children who had died. The first was Percy Bysshe, born in August 1957 (and named after the poet), who lived for thirteen months and died from hydrocephalus; the second, Margaret Ursula, born on April 14, 1867, and baptised in the Round House before her death from whooping cough on May 11, 1868.

The Victorians, unable to take photographs of their children, and wanting a lasting memory, sometimes called the photographer to the house to take a picture of a dead child. I believe that the photograph on this page is of Margaret Ursula. In Reeves' book it is listed simply as 'Mrs Shelley's Dead Baby'.

Barely thirteen months later Percy William was born and died on the same day, November 4, 1868. Arthur, who was five months on the night of the 1871 census, died on February 12 that year at Castle Precincts.

It appears that the succession of deaths

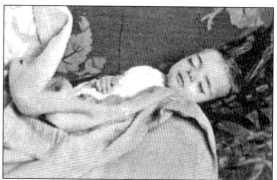

Margaret Ursula, who died from whooping cough aged thirteen months.

prompted Francis and Harriett to have the rest of their children baptised. *The Lewes and East Sussex Magazine*, in August 1871, records the baptisms of their five daughters at three separate ceremonies, Amy Alice on May 30, Harriet Mary and Elizabeth Frances on June 18 and Gertrude Margery and Edith Helen on June 29.

It seems strange that the children had not been baptised in infancy, particularly knowing the dire warning of the church that an unbaptised child would not be permitted a Christian burial.

By this time Francis had moved from the print trade and, in June 1871, been appointed Relieving Officer. He received a salary of £100 a year, a considerable sum that reflected the responsibility of the position. He was required to take out a guarantee bond that would act as a surety for the proper performance of his duties for the Union. His brother, Joseph Shelley, and friend, Edward Bailey, put up the necessary £200 to pay for this. The new position involved working alongside the Guardians of the Poor reporting on cases of poverty.

Among his duties were investigating applications for relief and support, giving emergency relief, sheltering paupers in the workhouse, keeping the books and reporting to the Guardians weekly.

Joseph and Emma continued to occupy the whole of 74-75 High Street with their family. Their eldest son, Joseph, aged nineteen, had already become a newspaper editor; William, eighteen, was working for his father as a miller and Fanny, Frank and Edgar were at school.

Harriet, nineteen, eldest daughter of Francis and Harriet Shelley, was living with her aunt and uncle and working in the shop – although she was also recorded as living in the Mill House on the 1871 census. This decade was a successful one for the milling and bakery business. Edward Reeves took the excellent photograph of Shelley's Mill *circa* 1870. It shows it in close proximity to Lewes Prison. The smock, no doubt with some repairs, was the same that had been removed from its original site in 1819.

Joseph, now a Master Miller, was rapidly becoming an important tradesman in the town. He employed five men, two boys and two shop girls.

Joseph and Emma's eldest daughter, Ellen, had married Benjamin Thorpe, builder, of the Cliffe, on July 29 1870. Research into a burial for an unaccounted-for baby who died on July 20, 1870, revealed that Ellen had given birth to a girl, Ann Thorpe Shelley, on July 13, 1870. The baby died at a week old from 'debility and convulsions'. It would seem that the Shelleys and the Thorpes quickly arranged the wedding when Ellen's pregnancy became evident. One can only imagine the feelings experienced in the two households during those two weeks. Joseph and Emma's distress that their daughter would bring shame on a family so upstanding in the community. The mixed emotions of joy and fear that the baby had arrived before the wedding and the grief that the family, but particularly the young mother would feel on the death of the baby. Did Ellen feel that she was being punished for her wrong-doings? Who carried the infant coffin to its burial place in plot ED 34 on that awful following day? Would Joseph have taken to the baby to its cold cradle in the earth or would it have been Benjamin, the father who had insisted that the baby should carry his name? And one last question – the wedding, by licence, was it a joyous day or a day tinged with pain and sadness? Maybe both.

A year later Ellen bore her second child, Emma, on August 2. Some years later Benjamin Thorpe entered public life and was one of the new councillors elected in 1881. He worked alongside his father-in-law, Joseph, on council business after Joseph was returned to local government in 1883.

A new workhouse in St Anne's parish had been built in 1865, designed by Henry Currey and built at a cost of

The Reeves photograph of Shelley's Mill c1870.

£12,700. It opened in 1868 with Mr and Mrs Rossiter as the master and mistress. The prevailing attitude was that the workhouse should be built in such a style as to present a forbidding façade with a harsh interior that afforded no comforts. The workhouse was built on the detached plan, which separated the different classes of inmates. Numbers fluctuated, with an average of 120 people accommodated. A school for forty children was built on the same site in 1875, with a resident schoolmistress. Those who now claimed relief would receive it only if they were inmates of the 'house'. The sexes were segregated and children taken away from their mothers. The diet was dreary and basic, and food was eaten in silence. A rigid timetable was adhered to from six in the morning until eight at night when the inmates retired to bed and the candles were extinguished.

As the years went by a more humane approach was introduced, albeit somewhat paternalistic. At Christmas 1871 Joseph Shelley, a Guardian of the Poor, with other guardians, attended festive celebrations at the workhouse. An *East Sussex News* report gives a rosy account of the inmates' Christmas Day, which contrasts dramatically with the well-known George R Simms' poem *In the Workhouse: Christmas Day* (or, commonly, *Christmas Day in The Workhouse*).

'On Sunday the inmates of the Lewes Union had their usual Christmas dinner in the large dining room, which was prettily decorated with wreaths, mottoes and festoons. Owing to a large number at present in the House a portion had to be accommodated in another room. A plentiful supply of roast beef and plum pudding had been provided and it is needless to say the dinner was thoroughly enjoyed.'

Another Reeves photograph, taken around 1875, shows the road up outside the shop at 74 High Street, as gas is piped into the premises. There are plenty of onlookers and workmen standing by. Could that be Joseph outside the shop with his daughter, Fanny?

George Shelley, at this date, was no longer involved with the family business. A newspaper snippet of March

Roadworks outside Joseph Shelley's bakery at 74-75 High Street, c1875. The shop is now Hugh Rae, men's outfitter. The bread ovens still exist in the building.

Above, Mary Shelley; inset, George.

bracelets. Her daughter Mary is photographed in profile, and in a dress that is freed from the constraints of the hooped skirt and the tight corsetting. By the 1870s fashion was changing and the crinoline was superseded by the bustle and the crinolette. This was made using half-hoops of whalebone sewn into a light material and was hung from the back of the waist with tapes. Mary, too, is wearing jet jewellery with a fine clasp set at her waist and gold pendant earrings.

Joseph Shelley, like his father before him, set up and ran a soup kitchen at St Michael's. In the cold winter days of 1871 it provided hot soup for 379 people of the parish. These were poor people

1870 reports that the licence on the Railway Inn on Friars Walk had been transferred from J Newham to G Shelley. However it would seem that George was not able to make a success in the licensed trade as the 1871 census gives his occupation as 'a retired innkeeper and out of business'. He was then living at 5 St Anne's Crescent with his wife, Mary, son William, aged twenty-one, working as a solicitor's clerk, daughter Mary and son George, seventeen, a printer's apprentice. Edward and Fanny Hide were at school and baby Beatrice, born to forty-five-year-year old Mary, was ten months old.

Both Mrs Shelley and her daughter, Mary, visited Mr Reeves' studio and two fine cabinet studies were taken. Mrs Shelley, in her late forties, is tightly-corseted and wears a full crinoline. One can only imagine the time and effort it took for women to dress at this period. She appears to be wearing jet mourning

Mary, daughter of George and Mary.

but not poor enough to be considered for a place the workhouse. The 158 adults and 221 children were fed for a period of ten weeks.

The 1871 census records Francis and Harriet living at the Round House but, later in the year, maybe because of the recent deaths of two of their babies, Francis moved his family to Castle Precincts, where baby Arthur William died four days after Christmas. Infant mortality remained high at that time, with as many as 153 deaths for every thousand live births. The veracity of statistics do not make it any easier for these two who must have been tortured with grief.

On September 30, 1872, money worries caused Francis to remortgage the Round House, again for £100 at five per cent interest, with Elizabeth Taylor, spinster, of the Cliffe. It was then occupied by a man called Rudwick, of whom nothing is known.

Tragedy came again for Francis and Harriet with the death of their third child, Elizabeth, who died at home on May 13, 1875, aged twenty, yet again from the tuberculosis that had plagued her for a whole year. Elizabeth was laid to rest in the St Michael's area of Lewes Cemetery.

Joseph Shelley was treasurer of the Lewes Provident Society for Medical Relief. The society proved to be most beneficial for the inhabitants of Lewes and the surrounding neighbourhood, in that it helped provide medical assistance and pay for medicines, for an annual fee of four shillings. It also helped to allay some of the fear of calling the doctor to the house when a member of the family was taken ill, knowing that his fees would be paid by the Provident Society.

In 1876 the Round House, still owned by Francis Shelley, was tenanted by Ebenezer Pannett. It is quite likely that he was related to William Pannett, the forage merchant and coal merchant who had moved into premises, in Westgate Street, below the Round House. The rate book, for that date, shows the gross estimated rental for the Round House as £13 and the rateable value as £10 10s.

Joseph Shelley continued to work hard both in his bakery business and in public life. He sat on the jury in 1873, was a Junior Constable serving with Robert Crosskey in 1874 and was elected High Constable in 1877 with John Maxfield Smith. Additions to the Borough inventory taken in November 1875 included 'a quantity of Ducks, Swans and Geese in the Pells'. In the following year, for the Borough Volunteer Fire Brigade, there were:

22 Brass Helmets 1 White Metal, 23 suits of Uniform, 23 bells, 1 Whistle and Chain, 9 Hatchets, 9 Hatchet Pouches, 4 pairs of Boots, 1 Oil Lamp, 1 Lantern, 65 Leather Buckets, 2 Iron Buckets, 2 Sets of Traces for Engines.

The Court Leet book of 1873 shows that Joseph's son William was keen to follow his father into local politics. He was nominated for the position of Headborough but was not elected.

Francis Shelley allocated another short tenancy to Thomas Christmas Bowen in January 1877 before he decided to sell the Round House. It was sold on May 28, 1877, to Lewis Smythe, a doctor of medicine, ending the sixty-three year connection with the Smart and Shelley families.

In 1877 a severe famine hit southern India. In Lewes, a public meeting to address the crisis was called on September 4, 1877, with Joseph Shelley, Senior Constable. The Earl of Chichester proposed the motion that the town and

Above, Joseph Shelley wearing the High Constable's badge and chain of office, with his staff of office on the table.

outlying areas would help raise funds to aid the afflicted. A committee was formed and money was raised and sent to the disaster area.

William Harry, eldest son of George and Mary, died aged twenty-one on October 8, 1878, from tuberculosis. His funeral was well attended with, the *Sussex Express* reported, several members of the Bluebird Troupe, of which he had been 'a corner man'. It has been impossible to find out anything about the troupe.

George, his wife Mary and their two sons, George, aged thirty-seven, who was working as a printer's compositor, and Edward, an engineer and turner, were still living in St Anne's Crescent. George was not as active in public life as his brother, Joseph. However he did work as an assistant overseer and collector of the poor rate in St Anne's Parish. These had been made paid positions from 1819 so George was still able to contribute financially to the maintenance of his home and family. His duties included giving temporary relief in case of real need, and carrying out the instructions of the relieving officer or guardians for those in his parish. As collector of the poor rate, he was responsible for deciding how much money would be needed in the parish to provide relief for those in need. He was then responsible for assessing the ratepayers and for collecting in the rate. George's name appears only once in the *The Town Book of Lewes*, when it was noted that he attended a public meeting on March 4, 1880, and volunteered to serve on a committee to help at a reception for the Volunteer Forces in Lewes on Easter Monday of that year.

Francis Shelley was working not only as the Relieving Officer, but also as the Registrar of Births and Deaths. In the early days, the registrar was required to travel fair distances to gather information from the houses where a birth or a death had recently taken place. It was necessary for the registrar to be literate, numerate and well-organised.

Francis, Harriet and their two daughters, Edith, a music teacher and Amy, still a scholar, were living in Castle Banks.

The Shelley women were dedicated to philanthropic tasks, not as holders of position in the public domain but beavering away quietly in the background. Any paid work that they undertook was of a gentle nature connected with the arts, music, art and needlework, although Fanny Shelley was a shop assistant in her father's bakery. Their voluntary tasks were mainly to do with the church, in particular, working with the children of the parish. The Misses Shelley, Amy and Fanny, organised an annual treat for 160 children of All Saints Church. The children had the excitement of travelling by train for a day at the seaside at Seaford. No doubt there was a hearty picnic, a paddle on the edge of the sea and the day rounded off with ice cream or a glass of sarsaparilla.

Francis Shelley arranged a day's outing for the inmates of St Anne's workhouse. What a treat it must have been for them, relieving the dull monotony of workhouse existence where every day must have seemed the same.

June 1881 saw an outbreak of small-pox in the town. To prevent the spread of infection it was decided that those patients with the disease should not be taken to the fever wards at the workhouse.

A Mr Medhurst proposed that tents be erected at the rear of the District Hospital for paupers. This proposal was seconded by Joseph Shelley.

Amy Shelley aged seven.

Radical changes to local government in Lewes came about in June, 1881, when a Charter of Incorporation was granted to the borough. As a result, the town enlarged, taking in South Malling, the Cliffe, Southover and the parishes of St Anne and St John–sub-Castro. A map showing the boundaries of the new borough of Lewes was drawn up. Away went centuries of tradition and of local power held by the Constables, Headboroughs and lesser officials. A mayor, aldermen and councillors replaced these ancient offices. Those of town crier, hall keeper and mace bearer were continued.

The inaugural meeting of the Council of the Borough of Lewes was on Wednesday, November 9, 1881. The men who had been elected councillors took their places and from their ranks, the first mayor-elect was Wynne Edwin Baxter, a solicitor who had also been the last Chief Constable. Then followed the election for aldermen – Messrs Walter Crosskey, Wynne Baxter, Thomas Chatfield, Caleb Kemp, James Adames and Joseph Farncombe were chosen. Lewes took its first major step forward towards modernisation of local government.

The Sussex Weekly Advertiser reported on a special general meeting held by the retiring Lewes Commissioners, prior to the handing over power to the incoming town council. Joseph Shelley chaired the meeting and the report records his skill in handling it and reveals his fine sense of humour.

The deed of transfer was signed by Joseph Shelley and W Duplock, transferring power from the commissioners to the town council and authorisation was given to pass the assets, liabilities and properties, previously held by the commissioners, to the incoming mayor, aldermen and councillors.

The Chairman wanted to know what would happen if they did not pass the resolution? What would the dreadful consequence be? (laughter).

The Chairman: "There is a great deal of vitality in us yet. I think we shall require to have a coroner's inquest upon us.

(renewed laughter). The Clerk has, I think, a resolution to put before us and I think a general body like this cannot go into the account as well perhaps as some of the members of the Committee. You will therefore, I have no doubt, trust the Committee a little longer to see that the transfer is done fairly and justly. All we want is that justice should be done to the town, and that the interest of each portion of it should be properly secured."

The new council had hardly settled into its new office when a controversy blew up concerning Francis Shelley. At a council meeting in December 1881 a letter had been received from him claiming compensation for the loss of office and salary. A report from the School Attendance Committee was also received stating that the committee had applied to the Local Government Board for permission to continue Francis Shelley in his position as School Attendance Officer, but that had been rejected on the grounds that a Relieving Officer could hold the post only under the direction of the Board of Guardians. In consequence the committee sought permission to advertise for someone to fill Francis's place.

It was reported in the local press that the Guardians of the Lewes Union had appointed Francis as School Attendance Officer for the whole of the Lewes Union, following the 1880 Education Act which made it mandatory for all children between the ages of five and ten to attend school. For this he received a salary of £25 per annum.

With the In-corporation of the Borough a large part of the Union had now come under the control of the town council and this had caused a reduction in his salary to £5. On these grounds and

Edith and Gertrude, daughters of Francis and Harriet Shelley, c1870.

on the assumption that he had anticipated a further eighteen years of working life as a School Attendance Officer, Francis would have expected an accumulative salary of £360. In consideration of this he said he was prepared to accept a figure of two thirds of that amount as compensation. The council, not knowing what was the correct procedure, decided to refer the matter to its finance and general purposes committee for consideration and report. Other officers had also suffered similarly under the reorganisation and it was agreed that all their cases should go before counsel for a fair and just opinion.

Counsel ruled that Francis Shelley was not entitled to compensation on the grounds that he had been appointed to his post by the School Attendance Committee of the Guardians of the Lewes Union and not by the local authority, and therefore the council was not liable for compensation. For a family beset with money problems this drop in salary must have caused considerable anxiety.

Then, after all fuss over his position as School Attendance Officer, it was agreed that Francis be appointed Inquiry Officer for the Lewes Union at a yearly salary of £5.

An inaugural dinner of the East Sussex Liberal Association was held at the Corn Exchange on December 4, 1881. About 250 notable members of the party attended, including Joseph Shelley. It was a money-raising event to provide a fighting fund for the next election where it was hoped to return two Liberal MPs in the eastern division of the county. Mr Barchard, chairing the meeting, declared that the aims of the association were 'registration, education and victory'. The press report of the meeting depicted it as a lively and enthusiastic evening with plenty of good-humoured banter hurled at the Conservative Party.

Joseph Shelley, with nearly all of his children off his hands, was now able to put his energies in to public work and service to others. The family business was booming and as a master miller he employed six men. Frank aged twenty-one, was following his father in the business and working as a miller at the Town Mill. The Christmas edition of the *Sussex Weekly Advertiser*, 1881, carried an advertisement extolling the benefits of his flour and bread:

WHOLE MEAL AND WHOLE MEAL BREAD—Joseph Shelley Miller and Baker, 74 High Street, Lewes, is prepared to supply the above, warranted genuine and manufactured on the premises, to any part of the town and neighbourhood.

Francis and Harriet Shelley 1875.

The St Michael's Almshouse in Keere Street provided a home and care for six poor widows or poor single women not less than fifty years old, who had previously lived in the parish for at least a year. Charity Hawke, who had attended at the death of Ellen Shelley in 1848, was given a place on the grounds that she was a pauper. Occupants were expected to pay threepence a week for each room they used and were required to inform the trustees if they intended to be away from the almshouse for more than twenty-four hours. They were expected to be model tenants; immorality, drunkenness and quarrelsome behaviour were not tolerated. The trustees were Edward Reeves, Joseph Shelley, Henry Saxby, Henry Davies, the Rector and the Overseers of St Michael's Church. Joseph Shelley acted as secretary at the twice-yearly meetings at the Black Horse Inn.

In 1883 Francis Shelley and his family moved to The Limes in Little East Street. This was a substantial house with two parlours, a study, four bedrooms and a dressing room. Outside were well ordered gardens, outbuildings and a stable. The house was large enough to allow accommodation to be made available for the registration of births and deaths and for his work as the Relieving Officer.

The Minute Book of the Guardians reported a meeting the year before when Francis applied for an increase in his money for maintaining a 'Pay Room' in his home. The Guardians agreed but only if the same room was made available as a vaccination station when required. Initially this was sanctioned and Francis was paid an extra £4. Later in 1883 the practice was discontinued as it was thought demeaning for the independent poor to attend at the same office as the paupers, who might overhear the amount of relief given to the former.

Prior to his election on to the Borough Council in November 1883, Joseph Shelley, as chairman of a ratepayers' group, strongly opposed the council's intention to buy the Star Inn and convert it to a town hall because of the high costs involved. He urged the council not to purchase the property until the ratepayers had had sufficient time to consider the proposal, and asked for a delay until after the election in the following November.

It was generally agreed, that with the incorporation of the Borough, there were no suitable premises adequate for meetings, public events, elections and council offices. A special meeting was called for August 8, 1883 when the case for the ratepayers' was heard versus a petition from those who were in favour of converting the Star Inn. Joseph Shelley presented a petition, signed by ratepayers from throughout the town, vehemently opposing the proposal. Among those who signed were Jonathan Jenner, a tailor living at the Round House and Francis and George Shelley, both keen to support their brother's petition. Although councillors were all too aware of public opposition, it was still felt that they needed to go against it. The owner of the Star Inn, WJ Smith, was quick to capitalise on the predicament and wrote to Alderman Baxter offering the building on 'very advantageous terms'.

Considerable communication followed between the council and Smith regarding the size and convenience of the property, the repairs and fittings required to convert it to a town hall. The council was unable to fund the purchase independently and needed to take out a loan of £6,900. In 1883 letters were sent to the Treasury in London to borrow the sum. But the councillors were turned down 'in view of the admitted hostility of the majority of the ratepayers to the scheme'.

So complicated and drawn out was the sale and purchase of the property that it took nearly seven years for all the problems to be resolved. The conveyance finally took place on June 27, 1890, and the Star Inn and the Corn Exchange were bought for £4,590.

Joseph Shelley was elected as a council member in November 1883. He continued to work with zeal and dedication to serve his community, rarely missing a meeting. He served on three committees – School Attendance, Swimming Baths and the Finance and General Purposes.

On April 2, 1884, Joseph Shelley proposed that a committee be set up to examine the condition and ownership of the Town Brook and the swimming baths, with a view to them being brought under the ownership of the borough council. It was decided that Councillors Parsons, White, Barrett and Shelley should be responsible for this task. The general consensus was that Lewes Swimming Baths should be fully repaired and an improved water system installed. Approaches were made to the Water Works Company to supply the necessary water. It was decided not to use water from the council mains. This had been tried previously and proved unsuccessful.

After further deliberations it was decided to purchase the sawmill in North Street from R Sampson – who offered the property and machinery to the council at a reasonable cost – and build there a pumping station that would supply not only the water for the swimming baths, but also public baths. It would appear that environmental concerns were already being established in Lewes as it was decided that fuel to operate the boiler could be provided most economically by using ashes from the corporation yard and general household rubbish. It was further agreed that the southern section of the sawmill could be converted to accommodate bathing facilities. A Baths Washhouse Act had been passed as far back as 1846, to encourage local councils to make bathing facilities available for all in order to improve hygiene in areas of inadequate housing. Six bathrooms were to be installed, four for the 'lower orders' at 1d for cold water, 2d for hot. The other two bathrooms were for those who could afford the necessary 6d. The total cost for the installations was to be £850.

The council recognised that the swimming bath and public baths would be unlikely to make a profit but had the foresight to realise that they would improve sanitary conditions in the town and benefit public health.

On January 21, 1885, there was a wedding in the Shelley family. Gertrude, Francis's daughter, was married to her cousin, the Reverend Arrowsmith Hide Shelley of Templepatrick, County Antrim, son of the late Reverend Richard Shelley, at Westgate Chapel.

Arrowsmith, born in 1862, trained for the ministry at the same college as his father had done. After six-years in Templepatrick the couple returned to England where Arrowsmith took up a position in Maidstone for three years. He died in the West Midlands on April 12, 1942.

The 1891 census, taken on April 5, indicates that Harriet, aged sixty-two, Francis, sixty, still working as a Relieving Officer, and two of their daughters, Amy, twenty-six, working as a drawing teacher, and Edith, twenty-eight, employed as a governess to a local family, were residing at 2 East Street. George and Mary were retired, their son George, aged thirty-seven, was working as a printer's compositor, Fanny Hide, twenty-six, as a dressmaker, Beatrice, twenty-one and a grand daughter, Ethel, aged eleven were living at 1 Abinger Place.

Joseph was still listed as a baker and corn dealer living with Emma, daughter, Fanny aged thirty-three, working in the bakery. Naomi Taylor was employed as a live-in servant.

But Joseph's health was failing and he was forced to cut back on his council work. He was diagnosed as suffering from diabetes. He struggled indomitably to maintain his position as a Guardian but slowly his illness became too much for him and on April 17, 1891, he was forced to retire from the Board of Guardians. He was unable to give time to his council work, his business or his work at the Westgate Chapel, where he had been both treasurer and secretary. On May 31 he wrote to the trustees and asked that he might be relieved of both duties.

John Every suggested that a gift be sent to Joseph in recognition of his long and valuable services to Westgate Chapel. A motion to this effect was proposed by James Broadbent and seconded by Mr Duplock. Mr Every was chosen as chairman of the special committee set up to consider what gift should be given. It was decided that a subscription should be set to enable his friends and colleagues to donate what they could afford. Ten guineas was collected and placed in a special purse. This was sent to Joseph, as an acknowledgement of 'the very great services you have rendered'.

Joseph left Lewes to convalesce with one of his sons at 77 Middle Street, Brighton. A fine letter of thanks was sent from this address in which Joseph said that he hoped to return to the Westgate Chapel as soon as possible. But that was not to be. On the October 7, 1891, the *Town Book of Lewes* and the local press reported on the town council meeting where the mayor announced that Joseph, 'having compounded by deed with his creditors' was no longer eligible to hold the role of councillor. John Buckman, the mayor, spoke

The Reverend Arrowsmith Shelley, with his wife (and cousin) Gertrude, and their baby.

warmly of the sterling, energetic work that Joseph Shelley's had accomplished both as a High Constable and councillor. 'He performed his duties with credit to himself and to the town,' he said. What a jumble of feelings Joseph must have felt – the ignominy of having his failing financial affairs exposed to all, being counterbalanced with the knowledge that he had such support from his fellow councillors and friends. The loss of face with his creditors, due only to his protracted illness, had totally debilitated him. The loss of his position and dignity as a town councillor, the effect on his business combined with increasing bad health, proved too much for him. Joseph Shelley died on May 6, 1892, aged sixty-nine. His death certificate, written by his brother, Francis, the registrar, gives the cause of death as 'diabetes, haemiplegia and exhaustion'. The report of Joseph's death, in *The Sussex Weekly Advertiser*, was brief and to the point.

'May 6th 1892, Death of Mr. Joseph Shelley of Lewes, miller and corn merchant on 6th ult., aged 70.'

However, the funeral service was truly fitting of the man. *The East Sussex News* reported that as the funeral cortege to the cemetery passed up the High Street, some shops were closed, others shuttered, and that blinds were drawn on private residences. The cortege consisted of a hearse and two coaches. As was the custom of the day, only men attended the funeral. Two of Joseph's sons, William and Frank Hide, his two brothers, George and Francis and two nephews, John and George, attended.

His son-in-law and fellow councillor, Benjamin, and grandson, Stanley, also paid their respects, with past and present employees and men representing all the important areas of Joseph's life.

On the Sunday before to the funeral, the Reverend C Badland, Unitarian Minister at Westgate Chapel, interrupted his sermon to refer to the death of his parishioner:

'An old friend has passed away who for many years was an earnest and active member of this congregation. All of the earlier part of his life, so far as my knowledge goes, was prosperous and happy, useful and respected. He was generous and kind, serving and helping many, especially those nearest to him, but also serving wider and local and public interests.'

The grave of Joseph and Emma Shelley, and other members of their family, in Lewes Cemetery..

77

Joseph's will showed that he was not totally bankrupt. Probate was granted in June 1892 and his effects of £266 4s 10d were left to Fanny Shelley, his daughter, with nothing left to his wife. Fanny was forty-two and unmarried. Perhaps Joseph felt that he needed to provide a home and employment for her.

On October 6, 1892, Francis Shelley, Fanny's uncle, granted her a fourteen-year lease on 74/75 High Street, which included the garden, and a lease on a house in Market Lane. All of these properties had originally belonged to Fanny's great-grandfather, William Smart. Fanny moved into the house and bakery at 75 High Street. Her mother, Emma, lived with her until her death in March 1896 from heart failure and chronic bronchitis. Emma was buried in Lewes Cemetery with her husband and two of their children, Emma, who died aged thirteen, and Joseph, who died aged twenty.

On a happier note, Beatrice, the youngest child of George and Mary Shelley, married Arthur Greenfield, a grocer. The ceremony was performed at St John-sub-Castro.

Harriet Shelley, living at the family home in East Street, was taken ill suffering from gallstones on the February 27, 1894. She died the next day when the gall bladder perforated. Francis wrote yet another death certificate for a beloved family member. Francis was to outlive his wife by ten years. The *East Sussex News*

Amy's artistic temperament drew her to amateur dramatics.

reported his death on August 10, 1904. He died after a long unspecified illness, it was written in the obituary, the last sentence of which springs a little surprise – he was a staunch Conservative. Somehow this revelation seems to be a contradiction of his family's and his own non-conformist way of life. His recently acquired death certificate shows that death was caused by chronic enlargement of the prostate and chronic nephritis.

While researching and writing about the Smarts and Shelleys I built up pictures in my head of how the family members may have looked, dressed and conducted their private and public lives. I became the onlooker into their lives. The men were easier, records of their work, their charity interests and hobbies give some idea of what they were like. The women were more difficult to imagine. Generally, those who survived to adulthood were married, the exceptions being Amy, her sister Edith and cousin, Fanny, Fanny Hide and Mary. Amy Shelley followed her father, Francis, into the Registrar of Births and Deaths in 1898. She worked from her home at 5 Dorset Road until she retired, aged sixty-five, in 1930. Artistic Amy entered Lewes School of Art as a pupil at fifteen and stayed there until she was twenty-one, after which she taught art. Little is known of her sister, Edith, other than that she was a music teacher, attended the School of Art with her sister in 1884 and was recorded as working as a governess in the 1891 census.

Mary, daughter of Harriet and George, appears not to have married although she has taken on the courtesy title of Mrs. She lived at 58 High Street in 1924-5 and next door at 57 in 1927-8 (Rebecca Stephens owned these two properties). Mary ran them as a bakery, confectionery shop and restaurant. However, by 1932-34 she is no longer living there.

And what of Fanny Hide, her sister? In her own quiet way she sprung the biggest surprise of all the Shelleys. Fanny had been elected to the Westgate Chapel Committee, giving her a status that she seemed to enjoy. Abruptly she tendered her resignation on December 30, 1898, as she was making an 'early departure to Tasmania' in the following October. Why she went to the other side of the world and what happened there is unknown. Research into the archives in Tasmania has drawn a total blank. The shipping lists for this period also fail to show her name. This lack of concrete evidence has thrown an air of mystery over Fanny's life. Did she in fact go to Tasmania? She was certainly back in Lewes in 1916 when she was recorded as living with her brother, George, at 57 High Street. She nursed

Edith Shelley in 1886.

him through his long illness and was with him when he died of bladder cancer on August 16, 1916. Fanny remained at the same address until 1934. She later moved to 54 Western Road and died there on November 26, 1949, aged eighty-five. The cause of her death was given as heart failure and senility. The death certificate has an air of sadness about it – her name is spelled wrongly, in the space for occupation is *'no occupation, spinster daughter of . . '* and there is a blank for her father's first name. She was laid to rest in the western part of the cemetery, near her brother George.

Through examining the Smart and Shelley men's roles in public life, I have a greater understanding of the workings of the past local government and a clearer picture of the social and working life of the people of Lewes.

What did I discover? On the positive side I saw a marked change in people's lifestyles, working patterns, health, education, and leisure times. This, for the most part, was due to the rapid escalation of industrialisation in the country, and in consequence, in Lewes, resulting in the development of new types of work, improved schools, further education, new housing, the establishment of utilities and the growth of the railways that allowed goods and

79

people to move more swiftly around the country.

The increased wealth in the town saw a growth in philanthropic works mainly through public subscription and religious affiliations. Shorter working hours allowed the working man and woman more time to pursue leisure activities. Families were now be able to spend a day out at the seaside, enjoy a picnic on the Downs, pass an afternoon at the swimming pool.

There was, of course, a down side; many still lived in squalid conditions and knew hunger, poverty, misery, illness and premature death, particularly of children. A hungry child, desperate to abate the gnawing of an empty stomach by stealing something to eat, could be severely punished, imprisoned and even deported. A woman, with or with-out a husband's wage coming in, made sure her children were fed by withholding herself from the meal table and making do with the left-over scraps. Large families squeezed into ill-lit, cold, damp, insanitary and bug-infested homes, that now sell as bijou cottages for unrecognisable prices. The old, the poor and the infirm struggled to exist, dreading the thought that the workhouse might be their final

Joseph Shelley in 1880.

Emma Shelley in 1880.

resting place.

There are so many loose ends. I wish that I could tie them up neatly and put a firm full stop at the end of the last sentence.

However, I suspect that I will continue to come across the Smarts and Shelleys in some newspaper snippets and have further glimpses into their lives for some time to come. I know that I have grown to love and respect the family for giving me insights into their lives.

I have a great sense of empathy with the Smarts and the Shelleys, who seem to have been decent, liberal, tolerant and compassionate people. They did their best to overcome their own problems in order to improve the lot of those who were less fortunate.

I feel that I know so much about them, as people. I just wish that I could have met them, spoken with them and got to know them personally. I feel that, through my study of their ordinary lives that I have become an accepted member of their extended family. I experience a sense of bereavement knowing that this will never happen and I will have to make do with staring in to the precious photographs taken of some members of the family.

NINE

THE LATER HISTORY OF
THE ROUND HOUSE

Pipe Passage is where clay pipes, in which to smoke tobacco? used to be made,
and boasts the house once said to be bought and sold within a space of a few days
by Virginia Woolf, a squat building, the bottom half of a truncated windmill.

Julian Vane

In 1877 the Round House was sold by Francis Shelley and Elizabeth Taylor of the Cliffe, to physician Lewis Smythe for £210. Dr Smythe was later to be one of the founder-members of the borough council when Lewes received the Charter of Incorporation in 1881. There was a sitting tenant, Jonathan Jenner, a tailor, who lived in the Round House with his wife and family. On the night of the 1881 those resident in the house were listed as Jonathan Jenner, sixty-five; his wife, Sarah, forty-five; their children, Edith twenty-eight, a housemaid; Percy twenty, a labourer; Eleanor, eighteen, a kitchenmaid; Emily, fourteen; George, ten; grandchildren, Ethel, eight; Sarah, eleven months; Jonathan's mother-in-law, Elizabeth Hollands, eighty-six; and tenant Henry Cooper, employed as a reporter. Was this a normal occupancy for the Mill House or was the family holding a census party?

By the time of the next census Jonathan had died and his wife Sarah was listed as head of the household, working as a laundress. Did she work from home taking in washing? There is certainly enough wind circulating around the gardens to dry a few lines.

The son, Percy, was still living at home, trading as a general dealer. On January 3, 1885, *The Sussex Advertiser* reported that Percy Jenner, hawker, was summoned for assaulting Thomas Costain, landlord of a beer house in the Cliffe. He was also summoned for assault on Robert Martin at the same place. He was found guilty and committed to prison for seven days' hard labour.

Also living in the Round House at that time was Annie, possibly a daughter, who was twenty-one, three children – Daisy, ten, May, aged one year, and a visitor, Owen Davey, eight. There was a new lodger, Arthur Bolt, who worked as a 'Sporting Correspondent'.

The 1891 parish records have an entry for a baby, Gertrude May, born to a single woman, Ethel Grace, living in Pipe Passage. Was this the eight-year-old Ethel of the 1881 census, and was the 1891 child, May, the baby?

Dr Smythe died at St Anne's House,

This unsigned, undated watercolour of the Round House (courtesy of previous occupants, Robin and Jane Lee), is difficult to date, but the costumes suggest it may be from the turn of the nineteenth and twentieth centuries. It shows the rear of the Round House, covered in Virginia Creeper. The flint wall on the east (left) is higher than it is now and there is no evidence of the two houses opposite the Round House, known to have been built in 1906. There is an euonymus hedge growing behind the flint wall. It is still there, but now stands at 8ft. The two large trees have been felled. The painting is a rather naive conversation piece and the eye is drawn to the five figures and a dog. Perhaps the person at the gate is Mrs Jenner, taking time off from her laundering, to have a few words with a neighbour.

Lewes, on October 29, 1906, by which time the Jenner family had moved out and Arthur Bolt – then in receipt of the poor rate – had become the tenant. Smythe's executors sold the house on July 10, 1912, to John Nash of 15 Grange Road, Lewes, for £180. Nash had barely moved into the house when, sixteen days later, an officer of the council called to inspect the drainage system. On opening up the well he discovered that surface water and sewage were leaking into it, causing a potential health hazard. Mr Nash was instructed to fill in the well and have new stoneware drains laid to the main drain in Pipe Passage.

The site plan shows an old water closet situated on the west wall of what is now the sitting room. It would appear that the job of removing the offending wc was not done properly for, some years later, Myrtle Broadbent, a child at the time, living with her parents in the Round House, recalls that the leg of the family piano, situated in that area, suddenly disappeared through floor boards that had rotted away due to an uncapped pipe.

After this initial disaster, John Nash lived in the house until his death on September 24, 1916. His will was proved by his sister, Sarah Woodhams and Alfred Wycherley of 60 High Street, Lewes, and the Round House was bequeathed to her and her son, Albert Woodhams of Hove. Sarah lived in the house for nearly three years but then moved to Brighton to be closer her to her son.

The house was placed for sale with Mr Wycherley, an estate agent, and in 1919 Mrs Woodhams showed the property to its most distinguished, albeit brief, owners, Leonard and Virginia Woolf.

Like something from a fairy tale . . .

Old Mr. Steggles' house was exactly like something out of an ancient fairy tale book. Instead of being square or oblong like most other people's houses, it was round, or, to be exact hexagonal (which is high-brow for six-sided). It was said originally to have been a windmill, and a stone announcing this fact was let into one of the outer walls. The roof – which somehow reminded one of a hat pulled down well over the eyes – two deep-set little windows overlooking the front garden, sloped upwards to a point, and in the middle was a large chimney-stack on which sat four well-behaved little chimney pots and one, evidently not-so-well behaved, to which a cowl had been fitted. This cowl resembled a question mark and gave a perky, inquisitive sort of air to the whole house. The very neat little garden was entirely enclosed by flint walls like those of the twitten outside; there were two ancient apple trees in a corner; some current (sic) bushes; quite a large patch of vegetables; a minute lawn, and a great many old–fashioned flowers and herbs, to all of which old Mr. Steggles attended with much loving care in rain and sun, frost and snow, biting East wind, heat–wave, thunderstorm and fog. The back of this peculiar little dwelling looked over what had been once the old town walls, now, alas, the proposed site for the erection of a row of very superior concrete garages.

From *In and Out and Roundabout* by Eve Garnett

TEN

THE WOOLF CONNECTION

Lewes that afternoon, with its many trees & laburnums & water meadows, & sunny bow windowed houses & broad High Street looked very tempting & dignified.
                                                                    Virginia Woolf

Virginia and Leonard Woolf, founder members of the Bloomsbury Group, owned the Round House for a very brief time in its history. Their dalliance with the property is recorded by them both as well as in many books written about the couple, in books relating the history of the Round House, and in books about windmills. I feel that it is worth collating all the information to give an accurate picture of their connection with the house.

In March 1919 the lease ran out on the Woolf's weekend home, Asheham House, four miles south of Lewes. As a result, the couple had to look for new accommodation, and they chose to to remain in the Lewes area where they could be close to Virginia's sister, the painter Vanessa Bell. Vanessa, her husband, Clive, their children Julian

The disputed cover design by Virginia's sister Vanessa

and Quentin and painter Duncan Grant lived for a good part of the year at Charleston Farmhouse, Firle, about seven miles from Lewes.

In May of the same year, Virginia had published her book *Kew Gardens*. At first it was not well received and by the end of the month only a few copies had been sold, which worried Virginia. During a visit to Charleston Farmhouse a quarrel arose between the two sisters over the quality of Vanessa's woodcuts, which had been used on the book's dust wrapper. Vanessa put blame on the poor printing of Hogarth Press, which further angered Virginia because the Woolfs owned and ran the Hogarth Press. Virginia did not take well to Vanessa's accusation that the press was not professional enough in its presentation.

She left Charleston

A collage of the Round House by Leonard McDermid, from Jean Moorcroft Wilson's book Virginia Woolf Life and London, a Biography of Place.

angry and upset about the quarrel with her sister, and worried by the nagging thought that they had yet to find a suitable residence to replace Asheham House. Her diary, for Monday, June 9, records that on the day of the quarrel she went to Lewes to view houses for sale. The first one she saw was the White House, at Culfail, a private residential estate on Cliffe Hill. This proved to be a disappointment, as Virginia disliked it for its pretensions. She wandered back into the town with three hours to pass before her train back to London. She visited Wycherley, the estate agent, and Mrs Wycherley suggested a property, newly on the market, that she thought might interest her. Virginia set off to view it.

Off I went up Pipes Passage, under the clock, & saw rising at the top of the sloping path a singular shaped roof, rising into a point & spreading out in a circular petticoat all round it. Then things began to go a little quicker. An elderly and humble cottage woman, the owner showed me over. How far my satisfaction with the small rooms & the view, & the ancient town walls, & the wide sitting room, & the general oddity & character of the whole place were the result of finding something that would do, that one could conceive living in, that was cheap (freehold £300) I don't know; but as I inspected the rooms I became conscious of a rising desire to settle here; to have done with looking about; to take this place, & make it one's permanent lodging. Perhaps it will amuse me to read how I went from one grade to another of desire; till I felt physically hot & and ardent, ready to surmount all obstacles. I liked the way the town dropped from the garden leaving us on a triangular island, vegetables on one side, grass the other; the path encircling the round house amused me; nor are we overlooked. In short I took it there and then, being egged on by Wycherley's hesitation & hints of a purchaser who had already asked for the refusal. Lewes that afternoon, with its many trees & laburnums & water meadows, & sunny bow windowed houses & broad High Street looked very tempting & dignified. The end of the story, which I must curtail, is that we have bought the Round House, & are now secure of a lodging on earth so long as we need sleep or sit anywhere.

Virginia and Leonard Woolf.

Virginia fell in love with the Round House. In general, the oddness of the structure and its setting overwhelmed her. As she herself confessed, she quickly became an ardent lover who had to have full possession of the beloved, wrote James King in his biography of Virginia. She decided to buy the Round House without even consulting Leonard, which perhaps reflected her defiant mood that afternoon.

There is some confusion here with the dates. Her diary records the viewing of the Round House on Monday, June 9, and yet in a letter to Vanessa, dated Friday, June 6, she adds, as a postscript:

I saw a house in Lewes on Monday and we've offered to buy it freehold for £300 – very old, small, but rather charming – however some one else is after it and has probably got it.

One can only presume that Virginia dated her letter incorrectly. It should have been Friday 13, 1919. Perhaps superstition prevented her from using this date. Quentin Bell, Virginia's nephew, commented:

It was an odd thing to do and an odd house to buy. It had been a windmill and stood high upon Lewes hill near the Castle Wall. Being in the middle of the town it was not really what they wanted at all. She returned to London in a rather defiant mood; she was always upset by a quarrel with Vanessa and by this time it is likely that the purchase, for £300, of a small cylindrical edifice in the middle of Lewes had begun to appear a little less crushing reply to her sister's criticisms of the printing techniques of the Hogarth Press than she had first supposed; nevertheless it was a course of action which had to be defended.

Leonard had not seen the house. What would be his reaction? Bell wrote:

He was in fact magnanimous, but they both realised that it was a mistake when Leonard was able to look at it a few weeks later.

In a letter to Dora Carrington, on Sunday, June 15, 1919, Virginia wrote:

We've bought a house in Lewes – on the spur of the moment. Its the butt end of an old windmill, so that all the rooms are either completely round or semi-circular. One of the chief decorations is going to be a large showpiece by Carrington, found in an attic at Asheham; doesn't that make you blush all over . . .

Three days later Virginia wrote to Vanessa, calling her 'Dearest', but referring again to their quarrel over the poor quality of the covers for *Kew Gardens:*

Did you realise that it was your severity that plunged me into the recklessness of buying a house that day? Something I must do to redress the balance, to give myself value in my eyes, I said; and so I bought a house; and blood will therefore be on your head.

Virginia and Leonard were to inspect their new property on June 26, she told her sister.

I'm a little nervous . . . of showing Leonard the Round House; I've rather forgotten what its like.

Then, in a letter to Lady Ottoline Morrell, on June 27, Virginia wrote:

We are down here involved in so many dealings with houses that we may well find ourselves bankrupt; and the first person I shall come to for refuge will be you, of course. But why, when we have just bought a house, should another one appear much more desirable —and how can one resist buying and chance selling?

While in Lewes, Virginia and Leonard noticed a poster advertising the sale, by auction, of a property called Monks House in Rodmell. They arranged to view and found it to their liking. On June 29, Virginia wrote to Vanessa:

We have just seen rather a good house at Rodmell, which is being sold on Tuesday. We are going to bid for it and if we get it we shall sell the house in Lewes. Do you think Roger would like to be told of it? If so, we would give him the first offer; some one else is said to want to buy it.

Her diary entry for July 3 notes that they discussed the possibility of buying Monks House and that Leonard found the prospect of the house most suitable but . . .

I, loyal to the Round House, murmured something about the drawbacks of Rodmell, but suggested anyhow a visit to the place; & so we went on. I think a shade of anti-climax had succeeded my rather excessive optimism; at any rate the Round House no longer seemed so radiant and unattainable when we examined it as owners. I thought L. a little disappointed, though just and polite even to its merits. The day lacked sun. The bedrooms were very small. The garden not a country garden.

Virginia cycled to Monks House the following day. She was not overly impressed with the house. The rooms were small, the kitchen inadequate and there was no hot water, bathroom or even a lavatory. However, the garden won her heart. She made a further visit, with Leonard. He, too was taken by the garden and they decided to bid for the property when it came up for auction, on the following Tuesday.

In short, we decided walking home to buy it if we could, & sell Round House, as we conjecture we can.

The Woolfs were successful in their bidding and Monks House was bought for £700. Roger Fry decided not to take up Virginia's suggestion that he might be interested in the Round House, and it was sold to John Every. Virginia wrote to Vanessa:

We sold the Round House, for £320, so we shan't lose anything over it; and I believe if we had risked waiting we could have got £400.

On August 12 Virginia passed her news on to Katherine Arnold-Forster:

We came down last month to look at the Round House; on the way up from the station saw a notice of an old house to sell at Rodmell; went in and bought it at auction for £700; sold the Round House for £20 more than we gave for it, and now in 10 days or so Mr. Gunn is going to move us in farm waggons across the Bridge to Monk's House.

In Leonard Woolf's papers, held at the University of Sussex, there are seventeen items of correspondence relating to the buying and selling of the property – letters between Leonard and the agent,

Wycherley, and letters to his solicitors in London. They show his fastidious attention to detail.

To Mr Wycherley, on June 4, 1919, he wrote:

We refer to our telephone conversation. I write to confirm my offer of £300 for the Round House, subject 1. the title being satisfactory, 2. The drains being pronounced satisfactory after inspection. I shall be glad to receive an early reply as to whether my offer is accepted.

The Round House was put up for sale for £325, but John Every's offer was for only £300, which was not enough to cover the costs the Woolfs had incurred. An increased offer of a further £5 was made and Mr Whycherley recommended that it be accepted as several repairs were necessary.

Leonard replied that he was prepared to go down to £320, but would not accept a lower offer. It would appear that John Every respected the Woolfs' need to cover their costs and the sale was finally confirmed at £320.

Jean Moorcroft Wilson, another of Virginia's biographers, said she felt that Virginia was so taken by the Round House that she may well have chosen to live in it had it not been for Leonard's desire for a country garden.

Perhaps, also, Leonard was further deterred from purchasing the property by the outside privies of the tenement houses just below the Town Wall, in what is now known as Westgate.

Let the last word be with Leonard:

Facts about the houses in which one lives during the whole journey from the womb to the grave are not important. The house – in which I include its material and spiritual environment – has an enormous influence on its inhabitants . . . But what has the deepest and most permanent effect upon oneself and one's way of living is the house in which one lives. The house determines the day to day, hour to hour, minute to minute quality, colour, atmosphere, pace of one's life; it is the framework of what one does, of what one can do, and one's relations with people.

Monks House, Rodmell.

ELEVEN

MRS WOOLF AND MRS WOODHAMS

A fictitious account of the meeting between Virginia Woolf and Sarah Woodhams

Whit Monday, June 9, 1919, Virginia arrived in Lewes from her sister, Vanessa's house in Charleston, near Firle, to look for a suitable property for herself and her husband, Leonard. The urgent need to find a new country home was brought about by Mr Gunn, the owner of their rented house in Asheham, who had given them six months' notice to quit, on March 1 of that year.

It was a quintessential English summer day and after the domesticity and tensions of Charleston, Virginia luxuriated in the freedom of being on her own to wander the secret twittens of the quaint country town. She stopped to look idly into the shop windows and over the walls of the heavily-scented gardens. Lewes was dressed in its finest holiday colours, bits of bunting criss-crossed the the High Street, still celebrating the Peace. The pastel-painted façades of the bow-fronted windows contrasted with the squared, knapped flints of St Michael's church. The Downs, resplendent in their fresh summer green, encircled the town. A heat-heavy somnolent silence hung, as if the town were under Sleeping Beauty's

spell. Virginia felt unusually relaxed and unfettered by the mild disagreement with Vanessa earlier over the wretched covers for her most recent book, *Kew Gardens*.

Virginia paused at the window of Wycherleys, the estate agent, and was drawn by an advertisement offering a most unusual property for sale, a round house, formerly the base of the town windmill. She decided to step inside and obtain further details. She was very taken by Mrs Wycherley's description of the house, which was newly on the market, but Mrs Wycherley was quick to point out that there was already someone interested in buying it. Spurred on by this news Virginia decided, there and then, to view the house.

Clutching the details firmly in her hand off she went up the High Street, reached the town clock as it struck the quarter hour and turned right into Pipes Passage. The air was abundant with the peppery smell of the tomatoes hanging pendulous in Kenwards' glasshouses, waiting to be picked. As she reached the top of the steps she could see, in the elbow of the path, an odd, queer-shaped building, nestling under a pointed roof which closely resembled a witch's hat drawn down over the eaves. To the rear a well-stocked vegetable garden clung tenaciously to the ancient Town Wall. The sun glinted on the small-paned windows and winked at the tortoiseshell cat slumbering under the holly hedge. As she approached the gate Virginia saw an elderly woman peering through the kitchen window, and presumed her to be the owner, Mrs Woodhams.

Mrs Wycherley had sent a note up to inform me that I was to expect a lady, a writer of some importance, who wanted to inspect my little cottage, with the possibility of a purchase. The very thought of such

Virginia Woolf

a visit fair threw me into turmoil. I was not used to meeting women of her class and a writer, too. I was unsure and nervous as to what we might talk about. I was in a dear old dither as what to do first, whether to change out of my gardening clothes and into an afternoon dress, or to rush to tidy away the pots and pans still on the stove from my earlier attempts at jam making. My mind did a rapid inventory of my meagre wardrobe and I decided that I would be more gainfully employed in the kitchen.

I watched from the window, gazing expectantly at every lady passer-by. I

felt a nervous tingle as I awaited her arrival. I found myself repeatedly ironing down the front of dress with the palm of my hand trying to remove the creases and picking at invisible balls of fluff on the arm of my cardigan.

I took a quick glance into the window that served as my mirror and scraped the loose ends of wispy hair into my bun. It was then that I noticed Mrs Woolf slip in at the rear of the cottage and sidle round past the japonica to the front door. I was relieved and need not have worried to the style of my attire, as she was dressed in a faded blue frock and wore a straw hat to shade her eyes. Her shoes were a little down at heel and in some need of polish.

Mrs Woodhams, an elderly and rather humble woman, showed me around the house, and I was much impressed and excited with its potential. It has an oddity about it, some rooms being semi-circular. I wonder how our furniture will fit in. It has a wide sitting room with a fire-place that Leonard and I will enjoy in the winter months. I went upstairs, where you can see one of the brackets of the old mill where the two houses unite as one. There are very fine views from the front bedroom windows right over to the

Weald and to the left I could see the Downs laid out like a patchwork quilt.

There is a vegetable garden at the back of the house and the front is laid to lawn with old-fashioned roses and honeysuckle cascading over the ancient flint walls. A dear path of old millstones encircles the house, laid out ready for us to play a game of hopscotch, a thought which I find most amusing. I feel that the house is cheap at £300 and it is freehold. I had such a desire to live there that I decided there and then to buy it on the spot without Leonard even looking at it. I am sure that he will like it.

That afternoon, Mrs Woolf and I took tea. I found her a little strange in her way of talking, but nevertheless, an interesting lady and I was most delighted that she liked my mill house. I felt that if I had time to get well acquainted with her we would enjoy much in common. The next morning Mrs Wycherley called to confirm that Mr and Mrs Woolf would like to be the new owners of my lovely cottage. I was much pleased at the thought of two writers living here, although a little sad at the idea of leaving my home. My son, Albert, worries about me so since my dear husband died and he wants me to go and live with him and his wife, in Hove. I am sure to be happy with them, but I will miss the garden.

Leonard and I went to take another look at the Round House, yesterday. On the way up the High Street to Pipes Passage, we passed a notice advertising a house for sale by auction in the nearby village of Rodmell. It was called Monks House. On reading the details, Leonard said that he felt that this house would be more suitable for our needs as it was larger and in the countryside, where we would not be disturbed.

We took another look around the Round House. Somehow, it didn't seem quite as I had imagined it. It was a sunless day, the bedrooms were smaller than I had remembered and the garden not really as we wanted. It overlooked some poor, cramped cottages, with outside privies and Leonard thought that the noise of the occupants might bother me. We decided to view Monks House in Rodmell.

I have heard this morning that Mr and Mrs Woolf have decided to sell the Round House on as they have bought a house in Rodmell. I feel rather sad as I recall how much Mrs Woolf enjoyed the thought of living here. I believe that Mr Woolf has changed her mind and maybe that she will regret this. Mrs Wycherley visited me this morning and told me not to worry and that there is another interested person who wants to view my cottage, a Mr Every of the Phoenix Iron Works. He will come this afternoon.

Sarah Woodhams moved to Hove to live with her son and his wife, but returned to Lewes and is buried in Lewes Cemetery.

TWELVE

THE EVERY OWNERSHIP

On August 3, 1919, the Round House was sold on to John Every, for £320, the vendor, Leonard Woolf. It was not bought for his personal use, but as a home for one of the workers at his Phoenix Iron Foundry in Lewes. Before Mr Every's new tenant moved in he spent time at the house working on improvements.

Novelist Alice Dudeney (Mrs Henry Dudeney), had bought Brack Mount (Mound) House and was having it renovated; she wrote in her diary on October 22, 1919:

Divine day . . . mooched round to look at my house, past Mr. Every's dear little mill house and he mooching around in that.

John Every offered the newly refurbished house to Arthur Broadbent, in 1920. He accepted and took his young bride to live there. Their daughter,

John Every

Myrtle, was born in the house and lived there until 1968, a period she remembers with much happiness. She still visits and has been most helpful in my research, bringing photographs and reminiscing about the years spent in the house.

When I moved into the Round House in late 1993 I thought it necessary to have the chimneys swept before lighting the fires. The sweep duly arrived and informed me that I had a John Every porch on the front of the house which, he maintained, could be identified by the styling of the window frames, both in the porch, in the front door and the door furniture. He told me that his house had a similar frontage and was one of Every's workers' cottages.

I have been unable to locate any plans drawn up for this porch addition but I do have the undated photograph, certainly taken before 1919. It shows the front aspect of the Round

93

The Round House in 1890, by Reeves.

House with a tree to the east, close to where the front gate is now situated. The most interesting part of this photograph is the entrance, not in the original recess which now holds the kitchen window, but on the other side of the building, seemingly secured by a flimsy and inadequate latch door. The photograph does show some form of early porch which would have served to keep the draughts out.

The porch is tiled with large quarry tiles, matching those on the outside. Near to the Every iron gates there are two utilitarian boot scrapers, certainly needed in the early days to remove any mud from the then unmade Pipe Passage.

In my search through planning applications for this period I happened upon one, submitted by Every on June 1, 1927, for an extension to the sitting room. This was granted and the exterior wall, on the west side of the house, was moved outwards by between four and six feet, making a significant difference to the room's dimensions. In consequence, the tower shown on the 1873 OS map, believed to be situated at that place on the Town Wall, was lost under the new foundations of the house. Richard Philcox – whose father bought the Round House in 1943 – noted that as a result of the new

Every bootscraper.

extension the rent was put up to £10 10s and stayed at that rate until 1943.

Miss Broadbent remembers answering

the door to John Every one afternoon. He arrived bearing a gift of an early print showing the Round House with a thatched roof (see page 37). He was delighted to have located the print and pleased that he could return it to its rightful home. I, too, am delighted to have the print hanging in my hallway and thank both Mr Every and Miss Broadbent for their diligence in procuring it for me and my successors to enjoy.

John Every had many claims to local fame, not least his ownership of the Phoenix Iron Works, which once occupied a large site at the bottom of North Street. Fine examples of Every ironwork can be seen at Lewes Railway station, in the decorative columns that carry the roof awnings, at Eastbourne bandstand, in litter bins at Temple Station in London and in the distinctive coal cellar covers and manhole covers around Lewes streets.

Every was a philanthropist who cared for the welfare of his workers. He introduced progressive changes in the running of the family business. He provided a Workmen's Institute, including a mess room for men who were unable to get home for their meals. He installed bathrooms where they could clean up after a heavy day in the foundry.

His benevolence extended to include his men's families; concerts were held, there were parties for the children, and a sports club, sports field and a pavilion were made available to his workers. He was a wealthy man and laudably used his money to benefit the ordinary people of Lewes.

I like to think that as he walked down Pipe Passage, from the Round House, his eye fell upon the then neglected Bull

Fireback in the Round House, carrying John Every's initials and the date 1919.

House that sits across the High Street from the twitten. He paid for the restoration of this fine building – at one time home to Thomas Paine, the radical thinker – and presented it to the Sussex Archaeological Society. In one of the main rooms in the house there is a fine example of a Phoenix fireback inscribed with a witty, but apt little rhyme:

Here stands the Bull within the West Gate,
Sir Henry Goring changed its state.
He built a house when Bess was Queen.
Which Westgate chapel since has been.
The Bull for Thomas Paine found room.
John Every saved it from its doom.

The Round House also has a Phoenix fireback, in the dining room; this is embossed with Every's initials and the date 1919, the year he bought the house.

A Phoenix firebasket stands in front.

John Every was a Unitarian and worshipped at the Westgate Chapel. In 1913, he paid for the old meeting-house to be divided, providing a reading room separated from the chapel and a vestibule as a reception area.

The reading room is now also used for the sale of emerging countries' goods and for the promotion of world peace, an ethos that would have met with Mr Every's approval.

He became a member of the town council in 1901, was mayor from 1903 to 1905 and became an alderman in 1906. He served Lewes for thirty-three years in different roles, always putting the needs of the less privileged first.

As a man with strong religious beliefs, he refused an order from the governor of Lewes Prison for his firm to erect a scaffold because he was strongly opposed to capital punishment. He also turned down an OBE in 1919, on principle.

After a full, active and generous life he died in 1941 aged eighty-four. The town came to a standstill for his funeral and memorial service. The Reverend H Maguire gave the address in which he praised John Every for being a man of vision.

He was hoping to see the dawn of a new order in Lewes and in England and in the world in which beauty, peace and order reigned in the hearts of men. John Every recognised his own weaknesses and those of us all. He accepted them and believed that the only way forward to his ideal was not through force and brutality but by the gentle, quiet peaceful and persuasive way.'

After Every's death his rented properties were put up for auction, at the White Hart, on Tuesday, August 17, 1943.

Alfred Philcox, a Lewes builder, attended the sale. He bought the Round House for £650, with the sitting tenants, Mr and Mrs Broadbent and their daughter, Myrtle. Mr Philcox had every intention of occupying the house himself so that he could be close to his office on the High Street and his workshops that

Christmas, 1961, Arthur Broadbent and his daughter Myrtle at the Round House.

were located just below the Round House, in Westgate. However, for various reasons this did not happen and the Broadbents continued to live in the house until the death of Mr Broadbent in 1968.

I never stop marvelling at the power of synchronicity. On a recent visit to Westgate Chapel I saw on the wall a brass plaque that read:

In memory of Arthur Clayton Broadbent 1878-1968. An Extraordinary Membership of 85 years.

It seems remarkable that the Westgate Chapel has had such close links with those that have been connected with the Round House.

The Round House was then rented to a series of students studying at the University of Sussex. In 1976 Robin Lee was granted a two-year lease on the house. He was a friend of Jane Brown, daughter of Rosemary Brown, who now owned the Round House with her brother Richard Philcox. Robin and Jane married in 1977 and made the Round House their permanent residence. Over the following years, with the birth of their three children, Tom, Abigail and Joseph, Robin and Jane needed more space than afforded by the Round House so they began their house hunting. I lived quite close to the Round House and after considerable stress for both parties, I finally bought the house in 1993. I have carried out extensive renovations to both the house and the garden to put my stamp on them. During the excavation of the garden countless little treasures have been unearthed and give me a sense of continuity with past residents, all of whom have made their marks on the house, as I have tried to do.

What of the future? When the time comes for me to leave the house I hope to hand it over to a new owner who will love and enjoy it as much as I do.

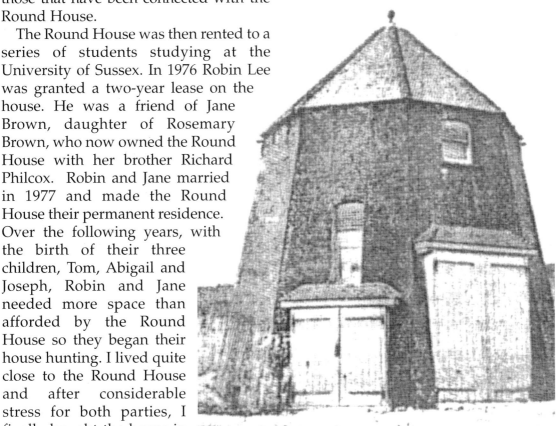

Rare picture of the round house of Shelley's Mill near Lewes Prison, after the smock was removed.

97

THIRTEEN

CONCLUSIONS

Well, the book is nearly at its end and I feel the need to pull all the facets of my eight-sided mill base together to complete the picture. I am honoured to find myself included in the history of this important house, located in such a beautiful position. It pleases me to think that the purpose of the Public Subscription Wind Corn Mill, possibly the only windmill in Sussex to be built for public use, was to provide flour for the poor in the time of dire need. I like to think that the original subscribers to the Subscription Mill were men of principle who cared fervently for their fellow people, and that in building the mill, they made a positive contribution to the alleviation of hunger and misery.

As I walk along the millstone paths and over the land to the front and rear of the house, I sense those who have trod these soils before, the Saxon sentries guarding the Town Wall, John French, John Bray's tenant in 1624. I think of John and Sarah Peckham who owned the site in the earlier part of the eighteenth century. Was it her steel thimble that was recently unearthed at the bottom of the garden?

Did Lord Pelham and the Earl of Chichester ride over to Lewes to visit their new land acquisition? As a vegetarian, I am not so sure about my feelings toward William Smith, the butcher who slaughtered his beasts and left evidence of his work to be found whenever I turn over the soil at the rear.

Did the early tenants of Smith's Croft remember to secure the gates on the new pathway at ten in the evening and open them again at four in the morning, as laid down in the original lease?

Did Jane Austen attend the ball at the Star Inn? She was visiting Lewes about this time. I spend many dreamy moments thinking about the grand ball and concert held in honour of the 'industrious poor', the fine Georgian dresses of delicate muslin, the rich red jackets of the gentleman of the Sussex Regiment, the music, the dancing, the fluttering of fans, the stolen glances, the chaises arriving to taking the wealthy Lewesians back to their town houses and country estates.

I think of William Smart – what did he look like? Did he have time to sit in a chair in the same spot as I am now sitting and gaze out of the window to the castle? Ouch, I can feel the pain of William's son Samuel when he crushed his fingers in the cogwheel. What happened to the poor boy? Did Frances blame her husband for not keeping an eye on their son?

How on earth did William Medhurst and his men manage to dismantle the mighty and weighty smock from its base and move it to its new site, at Race Hill? There would have been a few strong words uttered on that day.

I think fondly of the people who were born, lived and died in the house. Did little Gertrude Shelley play hopscotch on the millstones in the garden? Was a piece of heavy round clay, with a cross and four small indentations, found under the hedge at the front of the house, a plaything made by a mill child, or was it some kind of tally marker? I hold it in my hand and try to make a connection with the past. It is such a simple object but it is imbued with as much social history as many pieces that are displayed with reverence in museums.

There is no sense of sadness in the house, but how did Harriet and Francis cope with the death of their two precious infants who died here?

I look out of the window in my bedroom and know that Virginia Woolf experienced the same wonderful views across the Downs, to the castle and up to the Weald. I shiver with excitement at the thought of one of the greatest literary figures poking her nose into my broom cupboard.

John Every was a man of principle, a man who cared about the welfare of his workers and their families; a man well respected for his tireless work in trying to better the environment in which he lived. When I am pottering around in my garden, I can imagine him mooching around in the same spot. Every day I find clues to the past – pieces of domestic pottery, stems of clay pipes, oyster shells, lumps of glass flagons. Who was the last person to use them? How were they broken? I cherish these links with the past. As I ploughed through poll books, censuses, deeds and books in the Records Office, the Sussex Archaeological Society's library at the Barbican, the Lewes and Brighton libraries, I found myself

Plaque showing the Woolfs connection with The Round House, and a millstone showing the (incorrect) date for removal of the smock.

greeting the house's former residents as if they were old and loving friends, pleased when they are successful, sad when death visited them. I have enjoyed researching and writing this book and I hope that readers find something worthy of their time and interest in it.

Annie Crowther
October 2001

The author at the gate of the Round House.

ABOUT THE AUTHOR

Annie Crowther was born in Liverpool, but while still a child, moved with her family to north London, in 1947. She attended St Michael's Convent for Girls in Finchley, with her sister, Tina, and afterwards trained at Doncaster College of Education. Following teaching positions in both primary and secondary schools, she took classes in theatre studies in London and, with a group of fellow students, was sponsored by the Arts Council to travel to Russia and Poland to study and perform in children's theatre.

Annie then moved to Brighton where she worked with children with special needs at Hangleton Junior School. She was also responsible for the development of arts and crafts in the school. She left teaching due to ill health in 1981, and studied for a degree in social sciences with the Open University. In 1991 she completed a post-graduate diploma in counselling at the University of Brighton.

Annie moved to the Round House in 1993. Her hobbies include collecting bric-a-brac, particularly artefacts to do with childhood. Her creative talents are best viewed in the Round House gardens where she has developed ideas that are carried out by willing helpers.

BIBLIOGRAPHY AND SOURCES

Atkinson, DR: *Pipemakers and Sussex Clay Tobacco Pipes*, PBN Publications
Ayto, Eric: *Clay Tobacco Pipes*, Shire Publications 1994
Baxter, William: *The Cricketer's Guide or a Concise Treatise on the Noble Game of Cricket*, 1816
Beedell, Susan: *Windmills*, David and Charles, 1975-1979
Bell Quentin: *Virginia Woolf a Biography*, Hogarth Press 1972
Brent, Colin: *Georgian Lewes 1784-1830*, Colin Brent Books 1993
Brent, Colin and Rector, William: *Victorian Lewes*, Phillimore 1980
Brunnarius, Martin: *The Windmills of Sussex*, Phillimore 1979
Button, JV: *Brighton to Lewes Guide*, 1805
Crook, Diana: (ed) *A Lewes Diary 1916- 1944*, Tarturus Press 1998
Curwen, C: (ed): *Journal Of Gideon Mantell*, OUP 1940
Davey, LS: *Civic Insignia and Plate of the Corporation of Lewes*,WE Baxter Davey, LS: *The Inns of Lewes Past & Present*, Friends of Lewes 1977
Davey, LS: *The Street Names of Lewes*, Lewes Town Council 1981
Ellman, Edward Boys: *Recollections of a Sussex Parson*, Skelfington 1912
Garnett, Eve: *In and Out and Roundabout*, Muller 1948
Hemming HES: *Windmills in Sussex, A Description of the Construction and Operation*, CW Daniels 1936
Horsfield, Thomas: *The History and Antiquities of Lewes*, Baxter 1827
Houghton, John: *Unknown Lewes, An Historical Geography*, Tartarus Press 1997
King, James, *Virginia Woolf*, Hamish Hamilton 1994
Lee, Hermoine: *Virginia Woolf*, Chatto and Windus 1996
Lehmann, John: *Virginia Woolf*, Thames and Hudson 1975
Little de, Rodney: *The Windmills Of Sussex Yesterday and Today*, John Baker 1972
Meynell, Esther: *Sussex Cottage*, Chapman & Hall 1936
McDermott, Richard & Richard: *The Standing Windmills of Sussex*, Betford Publications, 1978
Major, Kenneth and Martin Watts: *Victorian & Edwardian Windmills and Watermills*, Fitzhouse Books 1992
Marler, Regina: (ed) *Selected Letters of Vanessa Bell*, Bloomsbury 1993
May, Trevor: *The Victorian Undertaker*, Shire Publications 1996; *The Victorian Workhouse*, Shire Publications 1999; *The Victorian Domestic Servant*, Shire Publications 1999
Morley, John: *Death, Heaven and the Victorians*, Studio Vista 1971
Moorcroft Wilson, Jean: *Virginia Woolf, Life and London, A Biography of Place*, Cecil Woolf 1987
Moore, F Frankfort: *A Few Hours in Lewes*, Farncombe
Bell, Anne Oliver: (ed) *The Diaries of Virginia Woolf Vol 1 1915-1919*
Nicolson Nigel: (ed) *The Question of Things Happening*, Hogarth Press 1976
Patching, J: *A History of the County Representation of Sussex*
Peacock, John: *Costume 1066-1966*, Thames & Hudson 1986
Pols, Robert: *Dating Old Photographs*, Federation of Family History Societies 1998
Powell, GM: *Windmills of Sussex*, Walker's Galleries, 1930
Richardson, John: *The Local History Encyclopaedia*, Historical Publications 1983
Simmonds HES: *Windmills of Sussex*
Smith, Verena: (ed) *The Town Book of Lewes 1702-1837* and *1837-1901*, Sussex

Record Society
Speed, PF: *Social Problems of the Industrial Revolution*, Pergamon 1975
Trevelyan, GM: *English Social History*, Longmans Green 1946
Vane, Julian: *Hope Cottage*, Hamish Hamilton, 1990
Wilkins, Robert: *The Fireside Book of Deadly Diseases*, 1984
Woolf, Leonard: *Downhill All the Way*, Hogarth Press 1970
Woolf, Virginia: *The Letters of Virginia Woolf*, Hogarth Press

Further research has included maps, documents and family papers held by the Sussex Archaeological Society at Barbican House Library, and by East Sussex Record Office at The Maltings. Also:

East Sussex News
Holman's Directory 1882, 1883, 1887
Kelly's Directory
Sussex Agricultural Express
Sussex County Magazine
Sussex Express and County Herald
Sussex Notes and Queries
Sussex Weekly Advertiser

ACKNOWLEDGEMENTS

There are so many people who have been an enormous help to me during the time I have been writing and researching this book – which started out as a pamphlet and has at length swelled to its present size. I would like to thank Roger Davey, Christopher Wittick and all the staff of East Sussex Records Office, but particularly Jennifer Nash and Pauline Colwell, who have been helpful, friendly and an absolute fund of local knowledge; Peter Hill of the Sussex Mills group (Sussex Industrial Archaeology Society) who gave me a working knowledge of the technical side of windmills; the staff and volunteers of the Barbican Library, particularly Susan Bain and Judy Brent, who have been so helpful and encouraging; Tim Cornwell at Baxter's; Pamela Day of the Register Office of Births and Deaths and Tom Reeves for locating and printing historic photographs.

My sincere thanks go to Colin and Judy Brent for reading my manuscript and making copious notes and suggestions; to Myrtle Broadbent; Jane and Robin Lee; Richard Philcox; Alan Ruston; John Bleach; Nick Flint; Emma Young and Susan Ridler, to Graham Mayhew for the photograph of Gideon Mantell's watercolour, to John Eccles, Sussex Express and to Alan Griffiths of Hugh Rae.

My special thanks goes to Judy Moore, my editor for her expert help, her patience and her good humour.

INDEX